What Others are Say

Amazingly open and authentic... this book is sure to be of help to legions of men and women ending long-standing relationships.

—**David Simon**, MD, Co-Founder of The Chopra Center and Author of *Free to Love, Free to Heal*

This book teaches perseverance, resiliency and forgiveness—and how to turn a breakdown into a breakthrough.

—**Lisa Nichols**, Star of The Secret and Author of *No Matter What*

Well written with a juiciness you will want to devour, and delivering powerful life lessons from one who has lived them, Farhana will take you on a journey to discover the complex emotions that one experiences during a breakup. Insights like this become a source of instant healing.

—**Jennifer McLean**, Host of *Healing with the Masters*

This strikingly authentic and enlightening memoir guides us to the real freedom that awaits us—when we have the courage to let go of what doesn't work in our lives.

—**Chris Cade**, Creator of *Liberate Your Life*

I have not laughed and cried so much over a single book since reading *Eat, Pray, Love*. This book is straight from the heart!

—**Teresa de Grosbois**, Founder of the Evolutionary Business Council

As a family lawyer for almost 30 years, I've witnessed countless examples of the pain and suffering when relationships end. In this very special book, the author captures the experience of divorce and turns it inside out, showing us another path: the ending of a relationship can also be transformed into a time of hope and an opportunity for a new beginning.

—**Thurman W. Arnold**, CFLS, www.MindfulDivorces.com

Farhana Dhalla shows us how to move from grief and despair to greater self-awareness and renewal.

—**Azim Jamal**, #1 Amazon bestselling Co-Author,
The Power of Giving

In this very powerful book Farhana Dhalla shares how to give ourselves permission to move beyond the sense of overwhelm and to a greater sense of personal power.

—**Rosalind Sedacca**, CCT, Author of *How Do I Tell the Kids about the Divorce?*

This book will awaken the wisdom of your heart and serve as a guide as you walk through the ending of a relationship and into the arms of hope and renewal.

—**Fran Hewitt**, Author of *the Ego and the Spirit*

I highly recommend this book; let it serve as your guide to find the divine in all experiences of life.

—**Karen Klassen**, The Enlightened Love Coach;
Founder of Women Embracing Brilliance

In *Thank You for Leaving Me,* Farhana Dhalla lights the way to a life of freedom, love, and truth.

—**Gemma Stone**, Psychologist

In this tremendously useful book, author Farhana Dhalla shares the importance of "owning our own response" to the ending of a relationship. This is more than just a good read—it is a pathway to healing. A "must read" for anyone seeking growth and happiness.

—**Ken McNeil**, Businessman

Inspiring, poignant and empowering!

—**Tina Cassidy**, Life Coach and Author of *Stop Holding Back*

A must read for cracking the code to having a rich, peaceful and joy-filled life.

—**Andre N. Mamprin**, Leader, Knowledge Architect,
The Next Institute

Thank You for Leaving me

Finding Divinity and Healing in Divorce

FARHANA DHALLA

BETTIE YOUNGS BOOKS

Cover design by Jarmila Takač
Photo of the author by Amyn Nasser

Bettie Youngs Books are distributed worldwide. If you are unable to order this book from your local bookseller, Espresso, or online, you may order directly from the publisher.

BETTIE YOUNGS BOOK PUBLISHERS
www.BettieYoungsBooks.com
info@BettieYoungsBooks.com

ISBN: 978-1-936332-85-4
eBook: 978-1-936332-86-1

Library of Congress Control Number: 2012955621
1. Farhana Dhalla. 2. Bettie Youngs Books. 3. Divorce. 4. Personal Growth. 5. Renewal. 6. Marital Separation. 7. Spiritual Growth. 8. Relationships.

Printed in the United States of America

Dedication

To the three inspirations in my life:

Tarhiqe, Meddyna, and Aiyeh.

Be audacious in your Magnificence.

Thank you for choosing me.

Acknowledgements

My gratitude and a long humble bow to the Great Divine for offering me this dance... for changing the music many times and being the masterful partner who swung me around with finesse.

All I had to do was surrender.

There are many people to thank and I am concerned that I may forget a few. Please forgive my momentary lapse and know that I value and honor your contribution in my life.

I am grateful that early on I would see my mother's hunger for knowledge. I witnessed her search for truth and her own painful yet exhilarating process of shedding and reinventing. With her as my role model, I longed to be of her intelligence, wisdom and open graciousness of "all that is."

My desire of wanting a "loving divorce" came from witnessing my mother, Meorah and my stepfather, Nurdin. They are pacesetters in living a life entrenched in truth and love. "Love under all conditions" is the mantra of my stepfather. He is the example of enlightenment in practice.

I am the luckiest person I know. I hail from a big, supportive, loving family who freely offer me guidance, share their skills and shower me with unconditional love. In particular, I offer thanks to my brothers Shabbir and Ghalib and their families and my massive clan of aunts, uncles and cousins.

I am immensely grateful for my in-laws from whom I have learned a great deal and for whom I hold boundless affection. They treat me like their daughter and are my family forever.

It said that if you have one exceptional friendship that lasts you a lifetime, consider yourself fortunate. Lady Luck must love me. Shaheen, Carla and Cristina, I have been able to count on you for unconditional love and devoted friendship, late night counseling and whoop-ass truth. You know the old saying: Some friends enter your life for a reason; a season or a lifetime... you are lifers. Thank goodness because I couldn't walk this life without you.

Then, in universally brilliant timing, these women entered, or re-entered my life and enhanced my world in immeasurable ways. Heather, you were the voice that inspired this book and without you, it wouldn't have been written. Deb, our morning coffee talks have guided me to new spiritual heights. Nargis, our daily de-briefs inspire me to see the Divine's hand in everything, and Fabulous Fabina—you made me your sister and my children, your children. I am so very blessed by you.

Whooshes of love sent to my sister-friends: Salimah, Munira, Farah, Janice, Shalla, Dorothy, Zeynep, Sheree, Christina, Val, Tammy, June, Georgina, Rejeanne, Kelsey, Lee with you is where I have my messy moments and still land safely. Thank you.

Elissa Collins Oman, editor extraordinaire, you breathed life into this manuscript. You saw the vision and removed all barriers to making it happen. I am awestruck and captivated by your innate knowing on how to coach me in translating my experience into a book.

Every author's fairy tale dream includes having an internationally recognized publishing house represent his or her book! Thank you Bettie Youngs of *Bettie Youngs Book Publishers* for believing in the vision and laying your golden touch on this work.

And finally, deep thanks to the father of my children, who loved me enough to leave me and was good–naturedly encouraging while I was writing this book.

Foreword

I never thought in a million years that I would read a 96-chapter book.

Yet what if the chapters were really not chapters in a book, but chapters in a *life*?

And what if those chapters were surprisingly short, wonderfully written, astonishingly authentic, incredibly insightful, and passionately pithy outpourings that could draw me into another person's moment-to-moment experience in a way that would benefit me as I encounter my own? Would I be interested then? You bet.

So here's the thing. The book you are holding is exactly that. And because it is, I couldn't put this book down. I read it in one sitting. I hadn't intended to. I didn't really have that much time when I first picked it up. Or I thought I didn't. But the book changed my mind about that. I am not kidding. I.could.not.put.it.down.

The secret of *Thank You for Leaving Me* is that it gets across major, *major* spiritual messages and gives us all big, *big* life tools, and does it without preaching, teaching, or screeching, interwoven as they are within the strands of a totally engrossing human drama.

Out of that drama comes wonderful wisdom on how to deal with the particular life challenge that so many people are facing right now: The End of a Life Partnership; the Conclusion of a Marriage; the Death of a Relationship.

Few events in life are more devastating. And when these things happen, people search for others who have had the same experience. "How did you get *through* it?" they urgently ask. "What happened to end it all and what did you do?"

Sometimes you can benefit more from a person who has "been there" than you can from a trained counselor or therapist. Especially if the one who has been there is open, honest, candid, self-aware, and, most important of all…has *healed* from their injury.

That's what you have here. Farhana's candid account is drawn directly as a spurned spouse's minute-to-minute experience that will keep you glued to the book and eagerly turning its pages as you watch another person's healing become your own.

If you are moving through the end of a partnership that you thought would last forever, I cannot recommend *Thank You for Leaving Me* highly enough. No matter the particular reasons your relationship shifted, the larger messages in this book will meet you where you are—and get you where you now wish to go.

I am so glad you are reading it.

Neale Donald Walsch

Introduction

I wanted to write a book.

Not unlike 98 percent of the population.

I thought it would be a nice "How to Have a Happy Divorce" kind of book.

But there were so many pieces I still didn't know how to do... and while we have a pseudo-peaceful divorce, it is not remotely close to the Club Med divorce that I had initially envisioned. I felt inadequate and hypocritical giving any advice.

Then, in meditation I heard a voice that told me that the book that wants to be written is the journey... my personal journey.

My journal, my trusted confidante, which had been capturing the play-by-play moments, would reveal the internal conflict, the road rash, the numbing fear and the moments of acute clarity.

I hated that voice on that particular day.

I was resistant... I didn't really want my stuff out there. I am an open yet private person. Yes, I know that sounds oxymoronic. But this was far too revealing for me. Even while re-reading the book to make edits for its re-print, I cringed at some of the experiences that I had written here. It's a little more skin than I usually like to show but I know raw and real is what really counts these days. In fact, 'real' is the only thing that really matters to me anymore.

Before you read this book, there are some caveats:

There are many sides to a story. I am not here to represent each side. I am simply sharing my own.

There is nothing linear about the healing process. There are times I have great understanding, am full of hope and excitement and then, in a flash, I am frozen in fear and burning in anger.

You might notice that I may have a discovery that may directly contradict the situation at hand. Such is the way... somewhere in the contradiction lays the truth.

All feelings of wisdom, pain, fear and love *can* exist at the same time.

At times I have been accused of making my process sound too easy. While there have been tough, retching moments, it was relatively easy. I don't want to apologize for that. I had a very clear personal mandate to make my divorce a loving one. And in his own way, so did my husband. I have discovered that if you take one step towards your goal, Providence moves two steps to making it a reality.

I have repeatedly heard people say that a crisis—be it illness, job loss, divorce, or another life-altering occurrence brought a gift that otherwise might not have been discovered.

At these junctures in our lives, the opportunities for re-invention presents itself. But, in order to re-invent, we need to let go of the old. We need to dissolve what we know. And then from the nothingness, arises what we *need* to know.

Please understand that while I have shared some of my story for context, I have no desire to speak ill of the father of my children.

My hope is that the discoveries that came out of the incidents will be more interesting than the incidents themselves. The incidents and the parties involved were simply catalysts to unveiling the greater truth.

Discoveries are always more important than the story.

After all, don't we all have a story?

What if our stories were entirely irrelevant... then who would we be? I would much rather live life from my discoveries versus my story.

One day, while sitting in the yoga lotus position, I asked God:

"Tell me what I need to know."

The answer came...

The lotus holds no apology or excuse for its circumstances. It blooms anyway. Tens of thousands of delicate petals open to unmask its beauty.

It gives, regardless of its situation. It basks in My love and opens in surrender to the Divine. In its surrender, it is a gift to all.

You, my child, are like the lotus flower. Surrender into your beauty, your fullness; this is your gift—your bloom.

The Lotus

Many Eastern traditions hold the lotus flower as a symbol for spiritual awakening.

The 96-petal lotus correlates with the sixth chakra—one of the seven energy centers in the human body. Located in the middle of the forehead, the sixth chakra, commonly known as the Third Eye, is associated with vision, insight, truth and holding the highest vision of self and others. When the sixth chakra is activated and balanced we feel confident in our own abilities and have no need to look to others to feel whole.

It is the journey of the lotus flower that holds the metaphorical meaning of life.

In the first stage of the lotus, it begins as a small seed down at the bottom of a pond heavy with mud and muck. In the second stage, the bud attaches onto a vine and grows slowly toward the surface. As the vine transcends through the murky water, the lotus bud continues to face inward. The third stage of the lotus is when the vine reaches the surface; the bud is kissed by the sun and blossoms into a beautiful flower.

The book is made up of 96 vignettes… each it's own petal of truth and realization.

This is the journey of my blossoming.

First Stage

The lotus flower starts as a seedling in murky water...

Even when you think you have your life all mapped out,
things happen that shape your destiny in ways
you might never have imagined.

- Deepak Chopra -

1

It was Valentine's Day. I had just found out that my husband of ten years had purchased a gift for another woman.

All day, I was numb. Surreally, I drifted through my day with heaviness in my heart. I hung onto denial like it was my last friend in the world. I couldn't bear the thought of my world disintegrating. It just couldn't be. He wouldn't do that. There **had** to be an explanation.

With a strange kind of calm that only complete shock can produce, I asked him about it when he came home. His convincing denials and the sincere look on his face almost had me believing him. For a flash, I thought I had manufactured this deception in my head. If I did not have tangible, physical proof in my hands to the contrary, I would have believed him.

The look of innocence on his face was familiar. I was shocked at how believable he appeared and wondered how many times in the past I had fallen for his lies. Clearly, I had just not wanted to see the truth.

After he had exhausted denial and he realized that there was no escape from the truth, he admitted purchasing the gift for the woman who had haunted our marriage for years.

There was relief in the air.

2

Over the years I would question him on things that didn't feel quite right about his relationship with her and he would look at me as if I was losing myself in an overactive imagination.

He would say, "You're crazy. We're just working together on Cub Scouts! Besides, she's married."

Now, with his admission, relief came from knowing that I wasn't going crazy. There had been something behind my suspicions these past three years after all.

He also looked relieved... from finally being free of the intricate labyrinth of lies he had woven. And now, he was free from me.

Even though the truth was glaring, I couldn't believe that my marriage was over. I asked him... no, I begged him, in desperation, for us to get marriage counseling, attend couple's courses or anything else to "save the marriage."

In a very evenly keeled tone, he told me he was done. He had already spoken to a friend and would be moving in with him. My voice rang shrill inside my frantic mind... YOU HAD A PLAN? YOU WERE GOING TO LEAVE ME?

Surprisingly, there was no yelling nor was there any drama. Lord knows we had done enough of that during the marriage.

3

Moments later, quite poignantly, our one-year-old daughter came into the kitchen and gave him a sweetheart candy.

It read "hopeless." Apparently, not all Valentine candies say sweet nothings. Strangely, we both laughed at the bittersweet truth of where we were.

Our two older children were in the other room and were seemingly out of earshot, but the enormity of what was happening could not escape their natural intuition. Our five-year-old came into the room and oddly asked if we were splitting up. Undoubtedly, the preoccupied look on my face all day and the quick flips from anger to tears had tipped her off that this was not an ordinary moment thus her unordinary question.

When we confirmed that we were going to "split up," she wailed a loud "NOOOOOOOOOO" that could be heard down the street. I didn't know then that this was the last bit of real emotion she would show for a long time.

We gathered our son and two daughters together and I calmly told them that their dad and I still loved each other, and would be best friends, but we didn't want to be married anymore.

I was irritated that he left it to me to do all the explaining to the children, while he sat there and wept as if he were the victim of this shocking decision.

left me to do the dirty work.

As I looked at my children and watched my husband cry while he was hugging them, I cynically wondered if these were indeed real tears or a set-up to make me look like the one who was exiting.

But I caught a look on his face that softened me and I thought: Perhaps there are no perpetrators. Perhaps there are only victims.

All of our reactions were so diverse. Our sensitive, soulful son was just six years old and struggled to understand what was happening. He asked lots of questions and was crying hard... he was deeply distressed.

Our five-year-old daughter cried too, but, in some ways, it seemed almost like a pretend cry after her initial wail at the news. In fact, once she even winked and smiled at me through the tears. And the baby just took pleasure in handing out Kleenex to everyone; completely unaware of how dramatically her world had just changed.

It was like I was watching a movie in slow motion. I felt like I had been given an anaesthetic and was witnessing everything, but I wasn't really a part of it.

I was poised and strong. The beginning of an act I would play for a long time.

A lot had changed in an hour.

4

It had already been an emotionally turbulent week for us.

Forty-eight hours before our fated Valentine's Day, a blizzard hit the city—an unprecedented six-hundred motor vehicle accidents had occurred. My husband was late coming home from work and wasn't answering his cell phone. I kept myself busy with the children, but I was growing anxious as the minutes passed slowly.

Finally, he walked in from the garage and a wave of relief washed over my body. He headed straight for the kitchen to dump out liquid from his truck console. I caught a whiff and knew it wasn't water. It was beer.

For years I had held my breath in fear, offered prayers for safety and felt tremendous shame in knowing that he would drink and drive. Friday afternoons were the worst. Every Friday afternoon, I would be at home with the children agitated with worry because I knew he would be at the pub drinking before driving home slightly inebriated and, at times, completely impaired.

But this time, he shocked me to the core. He was drinking WHILE driving... and on the most dangerous driving night ever recorded in our city!

I had shamefully looked the other way so many times when he would drink more than "a couple of beers" and then drive. I shamefully let him drive with my son in the truck knowing full well that he had consumed more than a couple at the baseball game. I had played ostrich

with my head in the sand and hoped his drinking problem would resolve itself. *he would snap out of it, get help.*

But now that he had detached himself from the welfare of his family
and disregarded his own life (and those who were on the road at the
same time) by drinking WHILE driving, I wondered why I had kept
so shamefully silent about it.

What was I protecting? An image? What about my CHILDREN?

5

This wasn't the first time we had discussed his drinking, but it
was usually in the heat of the moment followed by a couple of days of
coolness and non-communication.

After a restless night's sleep, I woke up at 5 a.m. to write him a letter. The letter expressed everything I wanted him to know and was no
longer going to play ignorant about.

Up until now, I had felt that I could "manage" his drinking. On weekends, he usually had his friends over and, because he was home, I had
let it slide.

I had a rhythm in keeping the ugly cycle perpetuating.

After dinner he would disappear into the garage and I would quickly whisk the children into the bathtub and get them ready for bed. By the time I came downstairs, he would be asleep on the sofa.

It is amazing what I allowed myself to adapt to.

But when I found out that he was drinking **while** driving, I felt flattened.

How could I fit that into the mix?

The letter was strong. I was calling out what I never had the courage to call out before—he was an addict. He was an alcoholic who put the lives of others, as well as his own, at risk several times a week. He escaped life and numbed himself from reality with his drinking.
I gave him an ultimatum.

Get help or the marriage would be over.

The next day, however, on Valentine's Day, the marriage was indeed over.

A part of me has always wondered if the final trigger for the end of our marriage was his love affair with the other woman or his love affair with Kokanee.

6

Two days after the decision to dissolve our union, the children and I left to visit my family. And he moved out.

When we returned home, everything was intact... All he had taken were a few of his clothes. It was hardly noticeable that he had left.

But there was a void. Hollowness rang in the home.

I was not ready to feel my pain; the numbness was safe. My logical brain kicked in and I started to ask myself some coaching questions like:

If we were to be apart, what kind of a split would I want to have?

What type of parent did I want to be?

How did I want "us" to be?

And from that place I started to create a vision for our divorce:

We are healthy co-parents with our children in loving, affectionate, safe environments—where questions, curiosity and ideas are entertained. The children are confident, have healthy self-esteem and feel wholly loved and totally understood. I am a role model of peace and joy. I know and love myself. The kids enjoy a healthy, joyful relationship with their father and feel supported by both parents at all times. Their dad is happy and moves through life with purpose and a strong sense of self.

I continued to build my vision with dreams of us always being a family.

I envisioned that we would reach the point where we would ALL take a family holiday to some Club Med spot... he with his partner and her children, me with my eventual partner and his children, and our three incredible blessings.

I held this vision with intensity. This was the compass to which I was set. I knew I needed a clear and compelling picture in my mind to help me steer through the anticipated dark waves of uncertainty and fear.

The ironic thing is, while I had a very clear picture of how I wanted my divorce to look, in all those years of being married, I had never really contemplated how I wanted my marriage to look.

7

In some strange way, I think I had planned for divorce most of my life.

I saw such a beautiful example of how it could be done through my own parents that I think in some subconscious way I was always prepared for it.

My parents split when I was fifteen years old. It never was a surprise to me... I often thought of them as being a mismatch. My father was a kind, likeable man, who was also a functioning alcoholic. My mother was the "strong one and the "wise one."

She remarried shortly after the divorce. Her new husband was a family friend and her perfect match. And while our "values based" community (and most of our family members) rejected their relationship and tried to muddy it, it was clear to me, even then, that this was what "Big Love" looked like.

In spite of community rejection, my mother and stepfather offered love. Through rejection from friends and close family members, they offered love. My mother cared for the well being of my stepfather's first wife. His first wife knit booties for my son when he was born. His daughters treat me like a sister and my stepfather has always held me in his heart like a daughter. My mother and stepfather were open-hearted and kind to those who rejected them and, some 25 years later now, all relationships are mended and no one remembers the rejection and grief... only love permeates.

Their vision was greater than the pain of the moment.

8

Armed with my Club Med loving divorce vision in mind, I kept it together, moving around like a vacant person with a counterfeit smile on my face.

The children's watchful eyes were on me every moment, looking at me to help guide them to understanding. It was like they were trying to grasp from me whether they should be afraid or not. Somehow the mask seemed like the right thing to do. It was the only thing I could do.

During those weeks, my husband and I saw each other and talked every day. He owned a plumbing company and we continued to talk daily about his business and I continued to help him with the quotes and any invoicing he required. This gave us practice at non-emotional, civil communication. In fact, since this was the style of communication we had been engaging in for quite some time, it wasn't much of a stretch.

Not only did I hold the posture that everything was okay in front of the children, but I presented that toward him too. I almost had a touch of Obsessive Compulsive Disorder in keeping up the appearance that everything was fine.

It wasn't until four weeks after our marriage ended and I was in the chiropractor's office for an adjustment that the facade started to break down. The chiropractor casually mentioned that a certain back massager I liked was in stock and perhaps my husband would buy it for my upcoming birthday.

Much to his surprise (and mine), I started to cry.

It was my first expression of tears. It was a controlled release, but nonetheless, it was much needed. The chiropractor was a little taken aback, but gently offered me kind words of support and the space to gain my composure. Then, I quickly scooped up my baby from the receptionist's arms and left for home.

It occurred to me that the ten minutes I was in the chiropractor's office were my first moments without children since the split. It was the first moment I could be a little real with myself about how I felt.

Slowly, I started to experience emotions other than those of a manic optimist. But expressing these darker emotions was still foreign territory. *Not like myself*

I was still afraid to show my anguish to my children. I wasn't sure if I could temper it reasonably and I was afraid that I would end up in an emotional puddle. My emotions were closely guarded and I kept a false state of levity to help my children feel a little more secure in the whirlpool of uncertainty.

Except for the tiny crack that opened during the chiropractor's office, I held it together pretty well.

Until...

9

One day, my tautly-pulled rubber band snapped.

It was the day he took the kids to the first function where people we knew would now find out about our separation.

He insisted on being the one taking them to one of *my* cultural functions!

I wanted to be the one to tell our friends. I wanted *my* version out there first.

I resented the fact that he hadn't spent any real time with the children since he had moved out and now he would take them around and act like Super Dad.

But what hit me in the stomach was that my children would be hanging out with "her."

She and I are of the same cultural community and she would be there with her husband and their children. Because of her and my husband's involvement in Cub Scouts, they now shared many friends.

I hated that he used our children as pawns to make himself look good and I cringed at the thought that she would be holding my baby in her arms, as if my child were her own.

I wanted to be there too, but I could feel my emotions unraveling and I knew I needed to take this time to be by myself.

As soon as I was alone, I was also alone with my feelings. My body started to do something I had never felt it do before. I became engulfed in pain. It felt like the agony of the past five weeks was finally overtaking me, and with no watchful eyes over me, I could succumb to my pain. *or Someone to hold me*

I sat on my recliner and wept... for eight straight hours.

The emotional dam had burst and, as I wept uncontrollably, I recalled the signs that I had ignored for so long.

Simple things that we needed his help with around the house had been ignored with no apology offered. We could have a leaky tap, a running toilet and a plugged garburator, but he ignored them. Instead, he spent an extraordinary amount of time at her house fixing her kitchen sink.

I painfully remembered the time he got dressed up for a Cub Scout leaders' meeting and the receipt I found later was for dinner and wine.

I recalled the Tuesday nights when I would be out teaching a class and would come home to a spotless house. I was always so thankful thinking this was a gift from him to me. Then, one day I found a child's toy that didn't belong to us. That's when my son told me that she was there the Tuesday nights that I was not.

With growing frequency he would suddenly disappear to return without explanation and when I inquired, he was either dismissive or explosive. Sometimes I would find him in his locked truck talking on his cell phone.

I thought of the time our five-year-old daughter stood up in the bathtub and sang, "Dad's going to quit drinking beer and become part of our religion." I smiled.

The conversation about conversion had never come up. Religion is a deeply personal choice and people have to choose a path that resonates with them. I thought it was a joke. Surely if he was going to convert to my religion, he would have at least mentioned it to me.

So, I casually told him that evening what our daughter had said, expecting us to have a good laugh.

He said, "Yes," he was, indeed, converting.

The other woman and her husband (who was also seemingly unaware of the extent of their friendship) were going to prepare him for the conversion.

I was stunned.

Had I become so irrelevant that something as significant as a religious conversion was not even mentioned?

10

I could not help the floodgates of assaulting memories as I replayed the time he and she took my son and her sons skiing on Boxing Day. He hadn't even told me they were going. I found out on Christmas Day from my son. I remembered how I had wept that day, knowing that she was becoming increasingly significant in my family's life and I was becoming less significant in my husband's life.

As I sat in the recliner, I sputtered out more wails as I torturously recalled the previous summer when my daughter and I showed up at a Cub Scout Family Camp. The look on his face was not one of delight. I was the intruder at this family camp. The two of them exchanged a look and then both carefully avoided me.

I wasn't amused to find them bunking together, but in order to "save face" I put on a happy one and acted as if nothing was wrong.

The final whip at that camp happened while I was loading the children in the van. I saw him sitting in his truck, seemingly waiting for us so we could convoy back to the city. But when I heard the wail of my son screaming that his dad was leaving, I noticed it was not us that he was waiting for.

It was "her."

He had left to escort her while I tended to our tired, now heart-broken children.

With my head down and my eyes averted, I avoided the looks from the other parents. The obvious was being stated and I couldn't bear to see their discomfort and their pity.

I remembered knowing in my gut exactly what was going on. The feelings of loneliness that had found a home in my heart dulled as the pain of betrayal took over.

But what the hell was I supposed to do?

I was four months pregnant with our third child!

I had wanted out too... but where was out?

I knew what was happening. And I pretended I didn't.

And now, sitting in this recliner, there was no more pretending... nowhere to hide.

I was leveled. I sank further into the chair in defeat.

I couldn't move.

I had wept so much it felt like there were no muscles left in my face.

I was broken.

Perhaps I needed to be broken in order to rebuild.

11

While in my marriage, I was tormented with the thought of this other woman in our lives. She seemed to be everywhere I turned. And I became increasingly frustrated with my husband, who turned on the charm and interest in the kids when she was around and then completely disconnected when she wasn't.

I burned with anger inside and out. The children bore the brunt of my unhappiness. I could see certain traits of my husband in my son and was especially harsh on him. I was so engrossed in my own tormented thoughts that, when the children interrupted my vicious internal dialogue, I lashed out at them with my repressed fury.

My dreams were restless and painful. And in my waking life, I was disengaged and I was stuck. Yet it seemed easier to stay with the loneliness I knew than to face the unknown alone.

There were times though that I was ready to face the unknown. In fact, the time that I had the strongest resolve to leave came just before I found out that I was pregnant with our third child. While the pregnancy was a shock, I always knew this baby would be a blessing. The pregnancy went well, but the time in our lives was tumultuous.

The moments that we did feel close were few and far between and the rift became greater as the pregnancy advanced. I recall driving myself to the hospital in my eighth month with false labor pains. I called him from the hospital to tell him where I was. He was at a baseball game and promised to come after his game. He never showed up. Reluctantly the hospital released me to drive myself home.

When I arrived home in the middle of the night, he was in bed snoring loudly. A sure sign of too much beer.

I curled up on the bathroom floor and cried. I knew then that I was going through this marriage alone.

We hadn't always been so disconnected. When I was pregnant with our son, I felt very connected with my husband. The Bradley Natural Childbirth classes did a marvelous job of getting the fathers fully and actively involved.

I suffered from terrible heartburn throughout the pregnancy and found that sleeping while elevated on the couch helped alleviate the burning. He hauled the spare single mattress downstairs and laid it beside the sofa so that we could sleep together.

Many nights we slept in our non-parallel positions holding hands.

We were a sweet couple from what I remember.

Twelve years earlier we met each other at a pub where our best friends were showing interest in one another. While we witnessed the possible budding romance between them, we got swept up in the ease of conversation that came from just being ourselves.

His charm and open adulation of me was intoxicating and while I was casually dating another more "suitable man," the boyish, daring, spontaneous side of him made me feel alive.

There was also a certain charm that comes from being an unlikely couple that attracted me. We had very different backgrounds and up-bringing but we were both adaptable people who enjoyed meshing our two worlds.

Many cross-cultural relationships suffer from lack of respect of one another's culture. I never experienced that. He was always open and embracing of my culture, religious practices and family. Yep, you can say his mama raised him well. His father was, and is, a gentleman. I have never heard a cross word or disparaging comment come out of his dad's mouth. From his parents, he learned traits that made him so darn easy to like. And besides, those dimples were charming...

We had been dating only a few months when he came over to help me clean the apartment for a party that my roommate, Carla, and I were having that evening.

I was busy wiping down the mirror when he came into my room to say, "I've just finished cleaning your bathroom. Is there anything else you want me to do?"

I thought to myself, those are probably the nicest fifteen words a woman's ever going to hear, and, in a spontaneous comical eruption, I asked him to marry me. He said, "Of course, Baby." We stood still for a moment and looked at each curiously to see if the other was serious.

We laughed and decided "why not?"

13

On our first real holiday together, we arrived in Montego Bay, quickly freshened up and went to the bar and starting chatting with anyone we met—not terribly difficult for two extroverts.

After observing us, the bartender said, "Two years."

Confused I asked, "What do you mean two years?"

"You guys have been married two years."

I exclaimed with enthusiasm, "Yes, how did you know?"

He said nothing and continued shining the glasses.

Then it hit me... we no longer looked like newlyweds. We had become distant even when sitting side by side on a tropical vacation. We used to be intertwined all the time—we used to hold hands and caress all the time. We used to sleep like a braided pretzel and would have happily sufficed comfortably in a single bed. In less than two years we had lost all that.

14

And now, here I was, even with him declaring "he was done" and the marriage over, I was still not ready to face reality. I told myself that we would only need a little time apart... to grow... to "find ourselves"... to come back together on new terms.

I could not bear to think of all the dreams I would have to edit him out of now. Every time I thought of a future without him, I felt scared. I was held hostage by my dreams interrupted.

I felt sad and hopeless. I was full of fear. I was fearful for the children's emotional well-being, fearful of our financial situation, fearful of selling the house and having to move, fearful of having to take a job (self-employment, while not incredibly lucrative, gave me the freedom to be a stay-at-home mom). And, fearful of being alone.

There were moments when I was immobilized with fear. Sometimes, those moments stretched into days.

I bathed in sadness for what was certain to be a lonely life. After all, who would want to be with a woman with so many commitments?

Three children (then aged six, five, and one) was a lot of responsibility to take on. And I couldn't trust anyone to love them like their own, could I? I was destined to be alone.

Unless of course we could work it out.

So, I convinced myself, it HAD to be him. There was no other solution. We would find a way. After all, isn't it normal to fall in and out of love in any long-term relationship?

And, according to him, there was no other woman. They were just friends... and he said that if he was guilty of anything, it was of not telling me of the present he got her—as a friend. Everything else was my overactive imagination.

It worked for me. I willingly climbed back into my cocoon of illusion.

15

In hope and a sense of preservation, I took this to be just a temporary separation. I wouldn't even let him use the divorce word. I couldn't allow us to speak of something so final.

I could not understand what I should do. How should I be visualizing? Should I be visualizing and concentrating all of my energies on us being together or should I picture us apart? And if I did visualize us apart then surely we would be... and then I would feel the weight of "Did we really give us the chance that we deserve?"

Heaviness sat on my heart as I muddled my way through weeks of anxiety attacks. Heart palpitations, racing thoughts and waves of fear struck me with no rhyme or reason and I became paralyzed. I was so afraid of a future alone that I convinced myself that a life with him was better than a life with me.

I asked God for a sign to let me know if what we were doing was the right thing. Perhaps this was just a test to make our marriage stronger.

Every time I wondered if we were doing the right thing, an event would happen that would make things very clear to me.

I asked him to come over to watch the children while I took a few moments for myself. I used that precious "me" time to grocery shop, which was a luxury to do without three children in tow.

When I returned home, the place was in shambles. Part of supper was on the floor, dishes were everywhere, toys had exploded throughout the house and his drunken friend had crashed on the sofa. He, himself was tipsy and seemed completely unaware of anything being wrong. All that in two hours?

My inside voice screamed, "You were here to BE with your children, to play with them, to love them, but instead you got DRUNK?"

I felt shocked, angry and violated. I muttered a few cross statements under my breath and took the children upstairs to prepare them for bed.

He and his friend spent the night; they were too drunk to drive. My son was excited to sleep with his dad as he so terribly missed him. He called for his dad a dozen times from the top of the stairs asking him to come and cuddle with him and after several empty promises of coming upstairs "in a minute," my son cried himself to sleep.

My heart broke along with my child's heart. I did not know what to do for him.

The next morning, when I came down and saw my upset house, I had a powerful realization. I understood why he didn't think anything was wrong when I came home to find him tipsy and the house upside down. This used to be normal!

His dismissive behavior to the children was, sadly, also normal.

And, just like that, the desire to share a home with him disappeared.

Although my head still played games with me for a couple more months about getting back together—all rising from my fear—my TRUE feelings were that I wanted a new normal.

I didn't want to live with him again.

The few weeks that the house was free of him, even in our confusion and pain, we had found some peace and security. I didn't realize how much until I had a glimpse of my old life again.

I saw the sign and it opened up my eyes, I saw the sign.

- Sheryl Crow -

16

We were all trying to figure out our footing with our new reality and with each other.

I felt like such a failure. I had incarcerated myself as a wife and as a life coach—how could I ask my clients to be truthful about their lives when I so clearly had lived a sham. I was at a loss with my identity.

The baby showed no discernable changes... she remained confidently the center of a world that adored her.

My son immediately took on the responsibility of the "man of the house." He worked so hard to be the one to shoulder more... and while I desperately wanted him to remain a little boy, I was ashamed that I had begun to rely on him so much.

Our five-year-old daughter, who was usually quite expressive, surprisingly, didn't cry. She didn't seem the least bit upset or concerned. She was a model child—no arguing, no explosive flare-ups, no back-talking...

A mother's dream...

Except I knew that she was modeling me and I didn't want her to lose touch with her truth the way I had lost mine.

She is a wise person whose astuteness can be quite remarkable. A friend once told me that when my daughter looked at her, she became nervous because she felt transparent and exposed.

Along with her uncanny wisdom, my daughter is full of life. Her natural, resting pulse is set at joyful, but had always freely expressed the range of her emotions.

For her to be stuck in happy mode was kind of "Stepford Wife" scary.

If she was going to model me, then I needed to give her a real person to model.

One particularly difficult evening, after putting the baby to sleep and as the older kids were brushing their teeth, I went into my room and prayed to God to put some peace in my heart. Tears squeezed through my closed eyes.

Then, I felt the gentle arms of my son wrap around my waist holding me silently.

And, a moment later, eternally curious, my daughter came bouncing up to me... "Whatcha crying about Mom?"

It was time for some truth: "I'm sad that Dad doesn't want to be married to me anymore."

"Me too," they both said.

We all hugged. With relief, we sank into a real place of admission for us all.

Not much else needed to be said.

17

My birthday was six weeks after our separation. His gift to me was a book—*Chicken Soup for the Single Parent's Soul*. I felt like I was kicked in the stomach. He meant well, but the finality of it all and the realization that I was, in fact, a single parent was still too much for me to take. I thanked him and cried silently to myself.

I spent the entire day in the bathroom with a runny stomach. I was feverish and achy. It could have been the 24-hour flu or it could have been the purging of all the toxic thoughts that over the years had found a welcome home in my body.

Now, it was time for them to go so I could begin my life with a fresh new slate. I could have believed it was the flu, but I chose to believe this was toxic release and actually welcomed the discharge every time I ran to the bathroom.

It's all perspective, I suppose.

In the midst of my stomach discomfort and the initial chards of pain I felt with his gift to me, I was experiencing a feeling of total gratitude for the children and the drenching of love they showered on me.

The words of profound wisdom that came out of their tiny lips let me know that God was speaking to me through them all the time.

And then, as I stayed in the warmth of the gratitude, something else began to brew in my belly... it was excitement. It physically felt the same as the anxiousness that I had been previously feeling but the emotional feeling was different... it was giddy excitement of what lay ahead. I had a profound sense of knowing that life was going to be utterly magnificent.

18

It was confusing.

We were together, but we weren't. Still intertwined in so many ways, we didn't know how to be apart.

We didn't amputate our relationship, but rather we unraveled each nerve one at a time, and gently gave it a little snip. Each snip meant a re-calibration. Some were painful... some were relieving.

In this confusion, I couldn't stop doing things for him. I was still grasping to save this marriage in some strange way. I wanted to be needed even if I wasn't wanted.

He used to come by the house every morning before the children woke up. We would have a cup of coffee together and then he would gather his tools and supplies from the garage and head off to work. I was very helpful with his business, looked after his banking, put out his vitamins, made him supper several times a week and even made his lunches for work.

This was ridiculous! I didn't even make his lunches when we were married!

Perhaps, I just needed to absorb what was happening to me in smaller bites and the illusion I was creating was a stepping stone to the truth.

But the uncertainty of the big picture was overwhelming. I had a hard time discerning what the truth was for me.
Until one night…

When I was fast asleep I felt a body beside me and the first thought I had was that my separation had all been a dream. And the first feeling that came to me was disappointment. When I found out it was my son who had crawled into bed with me, I was instantly relieved.

That was when I realized that I didn't want to be married to him any-more and then I realized something interesting…that while we had shared a bed for ten years, not once did I miss him beside me.

19

I was invited to a function the night before Mother's Day. It was my first night out since our split three months earlier. He came over to look after the children and they were excited to spend some time with him.

When I arrived home, I was shocked to find a babysitter there. After I paid her from my dwindling funds, I looked with horror at the state of the house. I had hired a cleaner earlier that day as a Mother's Day present to myself and now the place was a disaster.

When I went upstairs to sleep, I found a note on my bed written in my daughter's chicken scrawl printing saying "Daddy wanted to go to a party more than he wanted to be with us so that is why the sitter had to come over."

I was furious with him. How could he do this? Doesn't he see what he is doing to them?

The next morning I woke up with rage under my skin and an immense cloak of self-pity for cover. He was coming over to make brunch for Mother's Day and I was waiting to give him a piece of my mind.

The morning came and went without a word from him. As I started to get food prepared for us, I began crying in self-pity. The children just watched me silently as I wept. I reached for the only thing that was bringing me peace. My journal.

I wrote furiously about my ruined Mother's Day and within 90 seconds my sobs of self-pity changed to cries of joy. All of a sudden, I realized that Mother's Day wasn't about someone doing something for me; it was something far more profound than that. It was a celebration of God's faith in me to raise these children. It was in celebration of these children who chose **me** to parent them. It was a day to absorb the honor of the opportunity I had been graced with.

My children watched as they saw my tears change from despair to joy... all in 90 seconds flat. They smiled at me as if they knew that I finally understood the true meaning of Mother's Day.

20

I spent a good portion of my energy trying to find peace and love in my heart. I used affirmations and meditations. I did everything I could to stay positive.

But, along the way, I missed a very important step: I missed becoming a rage-crazed scorned woman!

I was in denial.

Denial disguises itself as comfort. Some turn to substances, gambling or shopping, while others jump into a relationship (or bed) with someone.

My comfort has been food. All kinds of food... sweet and savory have found their way onto my hips. I escape into a place of numbing love only to escalate the pain with shame in the very next moment. I have 50 pounds of denial on my body: denial of my beauty, of my ability, of my worthiness, and of my truth.

A big reason my marriage fell apart was because I was not honest about what I felt. I let things deteriorate. I didn't call him on the truckloads of lies that I knew he delivered. I wanted peace more than I wanted truth.

Finally, one day, I saw what I was doing and stopped making his lunches and stopped doing his laundry and began to wean myself off from doing any work for his contracting company. Actually, come to think of it, he was the one who told me to stop doing those things. Who knows how long it would have actually taken for me to wake up!

Without the maternal obligations to him occupying my time, something inside me switched. I became irritated with him. I was irritated by his broken promises, irritated by his half-truths, irritated by his lack of direction. His mere existence was annoying me.

I didn't want to talk with him casually, I wanted his stuff out of my space altogether. I didn't want him in my thoughts. I didn't want him in my house. I just wanted him to get the hell out of my head and my home.

21

I had a hard time integrating my Pollyanna self and my Chuckie self.

I had been so attached to the image of being a strong, level, confident, enlightened woman that I had never even given myself the liberty to be a psychotic broad whose fury would make any man who was practicing deceit anywhere shake in his boots and tremor in fear of castration.

It just didn't fit in with my Club Med vision.

I was angry with myself for not wanting to be a forgiving person and for not wanting to keep the peace "for the children" anymore.

How could I claim to be on a spiritual path when I was just so angry inside?

A comment from my stepfather took me by surprise. He said, "Farhana, anger is on the road to enlightenment."

That statement hung in the air before it slowly blanketed me. Then he went on to say "The spiritual path is about being in truth and that means being in truth about your anger

Of course I knew from the many books I was devouring that anger is a real human emotion meant to be experienced and then dissolved. The expression of anger is a way for the toxins to leave the body. To not experience anger means those feelings get stuck somewhere. That was the last thing I wanted.

Hospital beds are filled with people who did not show their anger.

Anger is on the road to Enlightenment.

- *Nurdin M. Kassam* -

22

The permission to be angry and the release of guilt around it seemed to offer me some calm. I was able to quickly shift back into being cordial. But still there remained much in me that needed expression—things that he needed to know. I wanted him to know how I was affected by everything. I didn't need him to respond as much as I needed to be heard.

Some months after our separation, as our wedding anniversary approached, I jokingly asked him what he was getting me for our anniversary.

He froze and then slowly asked, "Are we still doing that?"

I laughed and said, "No, but what I would like is for you to offer me your presence and receive me as I tell you what this whole experience has been like for me. You do not have to respond to anything. Only hear me. I know this is a tough one for you to do, but it would be the biggest present I could hope for and would really help me in my healing process."

I suppose that is why victim impact statements are given such high consideration in the court systems. And how an entire nation could begin their healing when the South African government installed the Truth and Reconciliation Boards to handle the injustices issued during the rule of apartheid.

He never did gift me that opportunity.

write it down — get it out
say it > optional
send it

23

Then, quite by surprise, the opportunity to give my victim impact statement presented itself in another way...

I was volunteering at a personal development course and was given the assignment to really express my rage. My friend Kevin stood before me as the representation of my husband and I unleashed all the anger and pain I felt from the betrayal and lies my husband had delivered over the years.

I let my fury rip.

My body was in full animation, my voice strained to be louder than the voices in my head and I let go.

Shout it out

For two full minutes.

Somewhere in those two minutes a shift happened. My rigid body relaxed and I could see clearly. Literally. Everything was crisp and sharp looking... like that fresh feeling of brand new eyeglasses.

Interestingly, Kevin had his own assignment to do while I spat rage at him. He was to act with "delight and glee." He was to ignore my dragon-fire wrath as if it had no bearing on his merriment as he skipped and pranced around while I raged at him.

This was a surprise to me. I had always thought that I needed to stick it to the other person in some way (you know, like a poisonous needle) in order for me to feel better. Apparently, it is not so.

Not only do they not need to be present in order for me to release and feel better, BUT they do not need to respond to me for the freedom of release to occur.

Huh! Who knew?

That night I drove home marveling at my clear vision. Literal vision, that is. I was reading the road signs for fun in total amazement at the visual clarity I was having. And my body, now agile and light, started letting out the most horrific gas sounds. I'd never heard anything like that before!

Later, I learned from energy healers that expelling gas is considered normal when there has been a big shift in thought.

I must have had the equivalent of a lobotomy.

I enjoyed the peace and clearing of the mind chatter that the tirade had given me. But, after some time in the relaxed state of post-anger expression, I started to feel something else grow inside me and once again began experiencing edginess and irritation.

I couldn't understand why anger was taking control over me again. After all, hadn't I released it?

It took me a little while to identify who or what I was angry with. And when I did, it felt like I had been sucker punched.

It turned out these new cauldrons of rage were directed at ME!

I reflected on the dysfunction of my marriage and thought: Why did I let those things happen? My silence was seen as approval, and on the occasions I did speak up, I was either dismissed as a nagging wife or I would suffer an explosion of fury from him.

But why didn't I call for truth on the many smaller lies spoken? Surely these paved the way for the bigger lies.

I was no victim.

I was an enabler.

Grrrr...

Betrayal is not what they do to you;
it is what YOU do to you.

-John Demartini-

25

I have always been drawn to personal development work. But I see now that when I took part in courses and workshops while I was married, I was always in search of how to "make myself better" so that he would love me more.

Ahhh... now I get it, wrong focus all together!

Because I was so obsessed with trying to make myself better, I never considered that I was just right "as is."

Every time I took a course, I would come home on an emotional high with a deep knowing that love was the answer. So, I would re-declare my love for him and my commitment to the relationship.

In the beginning, he would smile and seemingly entertain the possibility... but, in the last couple of years of our marriage, he would tell me flat out that he didn't think he had it in him to love me.

I ignored everything he said and told him I had enough love for the both of us and I would carry us through this patch—after all, wasn't this just a rough patch even though it felt like a sandpaper desert?

And off I went to another course with the intention of fixing myself or going undercover in a covert operation to "fix" him.

I felt like a tap dancer trying frantically to dance to a different tune with a synthetic smile saying, "Do you like me now?" "How about now?"

I didn't know whether I was to accept what was dying or spend my energy creating the possibility that we could be in love again. When does one actually check out of the relationship and what does unconditional love really mean?

In some ways the courses I was taking and the books I was reading confused me. I would often re-commit to the relationship with such passion and fervor and yet, at the same time feel that I was losing myself.

It seemed useless.

Then one day, after we split, it hit me... perhaps those messages about love were about ME loving ME more.

26

Those who knew me were often surprised to learn that I was unable to express my anger to him. I am quite an expressive person–one who usually plays the full range of emotions. So why was I so stuck here?

I reflected on it... I conceded that when we were married, the suppression was a form of preservation. It was not as if I hadn't ever expressed myself, as I certainly did, but my expressions of anger were tempered by fear.

I asked myself, what I was afraid of.

Accepting that he would not be able to work on our marriage.

The answer: I was afraid of him blowing up and leaving me.

It seems I had always held the fear of my partner leaving me.

not that pain again

But, in the beginning of our break-up, I still didn't express myself. Why not?

In some ways I was attached to the image of being the bigger person who always took the "high road" and I didn't want to stray from that illusion.

I was also beginning to feel hostage to my own Club Med divorce vision… my attachment to that outcome was keeping me in a false state of communication with him.

And another part of me was worried that if I did express myself fully to him, he would use it as an excuse not to come and see the children who so desperately wanted his love and attention.

Use it to not cooperate financially

As I was having these insights, I challenged myself to dig deeper. I realized that, despite my fears about his inattentiveness towards the children, he was beginning to show interest in parenting and was beginning to cultivate his relationship with them.

So, what was preventing me now from being truthful?

I realized that my financial reliance on him was what was keeping me silent.

And my silence was just another lie.

I had continued to let things slide, as I had done in the past. I hadn't called him on the obvious and trivial lies that he was so adept at dishing out to me. Nor had I held him responsible for his many broken commitments to the children.

It was clear that I needed my own financial independence as a vehicle to speaking my truth.

I needed a divorce agreement to at least hold him accountable for child support. But that meant that I would need to accept that divorce was indeed the solution for us. The thought of moving towards divorce landed like a thud in my stomach.

27

The first time I saw my girlfriends after they found out about the split they struggled to make eye contact with me and avoided chatting with me.

I was shocked.

Here I thought I would have support, a shoulder to lean on... not so.

It was reminiscent of when I was a teenager and my parents divorced. People suddenly stopped speaking to us. I would scream inside, "It's not contagious!" and now 25 years later the sudden avoidance from people reminded me of the abandonment that I experienced as a teenager and I felt afraid.

On the way home after seeing my girlfriends, I was crying and my mother who was visiting at that time offered these words to me:

"Farhana, they don't know what to say. Regrettably, the same thing would have happened if you had said you had cancer. People don't know how to react with that kind of information. Besides, you both seemed so happy. So, when they see it happen to you, it makes them contemplate the fragility of their own marriages. Show them compassion, Sweetie."

Show THEM compassion? Come on! I was annoyed at being asked to take the high road for them—supposedly my closest friends. I felt completely unsupported and my feelings dismissed.

For a few hours, I held the pain and hurt, but by the time I went to sleep that evening, I found myself sending them compassion for their fear and, amazingly, my pain subsided.

If you want others to be happy, practice compassion. If you want to be happy, practice compassion.

- His Holiness, The Dalai Lama -

28

I have confusion about who he is to me. He is not my husband anymore and that is okay... he'll never be just an acquaintance... but he is something more than just a friend. I just don't know what that is yet...

I miss my name. His last name was my middle name. It looked good. It flowed.

Symbolically, to cut off any energetic ties to being married to him, I dropped his name. I was sad to do it.

After I dropped his last name as my middle name—a relatively easy task as I had never taken it legally—my daughter asked me why I didn't use it anymore. I told her that I was still a Dhalla. I always had been. I had never taken his name for real.

Her eyes opened and she incredulously stated, "Well, then that explains everything!"

29

Shortly before we split up, I had seen an Al-Anon advertisement in the local paper. Finally, some place where I could go to for relief, I thought. There were only four of us at the meeting, and as a new-comer they gave me lots of airtime, which I gladly took.

I thought they would commiserate with my misery and agree to what a jerk my husband was. But they patiently listened and said nothing. So, to be sure they heard me, I spoke louder and gave more examples of how uncaring and self-absorbed my husband was. They just listened.

I was frustrated. I decided that if they couldn't at least validate that he was being a jerk, then I wasn't going back to another meeting. I wanted my pain to be validated so badly that I just wasn't willing to let go of my position of being "right."

A couple of weeks later, I attended a personal development program and the Master Trainer said something to the group that hit me to the core. He said that I was with my energetic equivalent. That at some point in time, I intentionally matched up with him as he fulfilled all the pieces of my own discontentment.

We were both escape artists. I escaped into food and busy-ness. He, into alcohol and other people. We were both hurting. We were trying to numb our inner pain with others and seek validation from others.

I had spent so much time highlighting the differences between us that it pained me to see that we were so similar.

30

We have become vegetarians well, not really. But ever since he left and the BBQ went along with him, cooking meat seems like a rather unappealing task. Even if the BBQ had remained, it would have been a garden ornament, as I have no clue how to light it.

For such a competent woman, there are many areas in which I fail miserably... areas where I love being taken care of. And it is here that I came to notice the things around the house that he had taken care of.

That first summer, I noticed the lawn needed cutting and I didn't know where the lawn mower was kept... or even if we had one! I felt like a charity case... helplessly looking at the long grass until I became the recipient of the generosity of our good neighbors, a dear girlfriend... and yes, sometimes even he mowed it for me.

The following summer, my son stepped into that responsibility and many of my new girlfriends were very efficient at a number of things and were generous with sharing their time and knowledge with me.

Interestingly, even though there was more work to be done, things were less arduous. I wondered why that was so.

I came to recognize that I was not waiting for him to do something, then nagging him to complete it, then getting angry that it wasn't done, then telling myself he didn't care about me, and then withholding my love and affection.

I had wasted so much energy complaining and depleting my happiness by telling myself awful stories about how little he cared about me. Yet, when I just did the work myself, it was rather easy and I felt good taking care of our home.

There is an ease and freedom that comes from not having any expectations on anyone else.

31

One day I woke up with pain all over my body. But it was a strange pain. It had no location. It was everywhere and trapped as painful sadness in my cells. I was in a symphony of pain, yet numb.

I drove on autopilot to the Traditional Chinese Healing Centre, a place I had never been to before, and just looked at the lady and said, "Help me."

She looked deeply into my eyes and then nodded. She gave me a form to fill out. I put the right date on the form but noticed I had put the wrong year. I erroneously put our wedding year—it was our anniversary. When I saw what I had written, I sobbed... and couldn't stop. She did some acupuncture on me and offered me comfort while I wept and wailed in the room for an hour. Luckily, I was the only patient there and she allowed me the freedom to release the deep sadness that was stuck in my body.

And then I went home and ate a box of cookies.

32

I knew that, even in the deep pain, I was not entertaining a life with him again. I was mourning the death of a dream. I was mourning for him as I was for myself.

There was still a lot of compassion and humanity between us, and I knew on some deep level what I was experiencing was a new form of love for him. I couldn't articulate it at the time, but I knew that my heart was blowing open with love.

The next morning as I went into my meditation—at least that is what I call it, I have no clue if I am doing it right or not—I had an interesting thought.

I have always held an internal smugness that I was the more evolved soul in the relationship. Then, in a twist, I asked myself, what if he were the more evolved soul that came to give me these lessons for my evolution?

And suddenly, with that paradigm shift, I understood his profound love for me on a soul level.

I now understood the context of the immense love that I had been cultivating towards him.

A gift for me to learn & evolve.

Second Stage

*The tiny lotus bud attaches onto a vine and faces inward
as it journeys up to the surface...*

If you are going through a crisis,
something more wants to manifest.

- Kute Blackson -

33

In my marriage, I spent an extraordinary amount of time painting this picture of what was possible, telling him how much I believed in him, fixing his work and then nagging him on the things he had not done. You know, like a coach/cheerleader/neurotic mom.

I attached so many dreams onto him.

I did all this to keep from looking at me.

I used him as a distraction.

And now that I had to think about my own possibilities, my dreams, my life, I felt incapacitated like I didn't even know how to think. Everything I thought I knew, everything I thought I wanted, seemed to be dissolving at such a rapid pace.

My mandate now seemed to be both dismantling and creating new thoughts, beliefs and dreams. It felt like I had built a sandcastle and the waves came in and swept it away. There was sadness at seeing it all dissolve in front of my eyes.

There was still temptation to try and salvage the melted sand, but I also knew that I would be far better off starting anew on higher ground.

Every day I had to recommit to the break-up. I had to remind myself that this was the right thing. In the beginning, it felt like all my dreams and wishes had been interrupted and I struggled to make sense with "What now?"

But as I started to visualize and create this new life, the haunting memories of "what could have been" started to fade away.

Was I really mourning the relationship or my dreams of what I thought it held?

34

I was furiously brushing my hair and angrily muttering under my breath in a fictitious conversation in my head with him. I stopped and asked God for help to get me centered.

Just then, I listened as my daughter said to her little sister, "Let's go Lifeboarding."

Curious, I asked her what Lifeboarding was. She said, "Remember what we were doing yesterday when we were dreaming about the house we wanted and where we want to go traveling? That is Lifeboarding."

A vision instantly appeared in my mind. I knew that word was going to be a segment in a book. And then a nano-second later, I understood that I was to become the writer of that book. A pretty bold vision for someone who had never even written an article.

The clear message to me then, and now, remains: dream and create pictures of what I want the future to look like so I can take my head out of the dark clouds of the present and feel "possible" again.

And from this place of possibility, I began to create.

My daughter and I would dream-build together... adding more lushness and detail into our wishes. It was a delightful escape into wonderland.

Lifeboarding... nice...

now have a vision board on the wall in front of my desk.

In fact, my whole office is filled with vision boards...LifeBoards actually. They keep me afloat when I think I am sinking.

Creating them has been part of my re-creation process... to surround myself with images that bring me joy.

I had been so caught up in my mom/wife identity that, along the way, I lost who I was as an individual.

This process of **me** choosing **me** was a little unnerving. I was surprised by how much I didn't know about what I truly wanted. Who did I want to re-invent myself to be? Assuming I could have it all, what would I pick?

I knew there was tremendous power in visualization. The testimonies are in every book, from healing to making money and parenting to public speaking. The power of visualization could not be in question any longer.

So I tore pictures out of magazines to help me excavate who I was and remember what used to rock my world and what used to bring me joy... and what was bringing me joy now. I didn't second-guess or censor my wishes or weigh them... I decided to take out a membership in the "I Want it All" Club.

I was ready to try something new...and besides...as we excitedly tore out the words and images that represented our dreams, the kids and I agreed that cutting and pasting (and dreaming) is fun.

I dream my painting and then I paint my dream.

- Vincent Van Gogh -

36

A friend of mine once told me that she was rather unimpressed with my lack of revenge and rage.

She shared with me the intricate revenge plan she had plotted out when her marriage went sideways and she was surprised at my lack of connection to the heat and fury of it all.

It did make me wonder if I was just suppressing my rage under the guise of spiritual enlightenment.

What if I go postal on everyone one day? That would just suck.

It's not like I didn't ever think about it… I struggled all the time between wanting to have an "evolved" parting and being seduced by the glittery lights of revenge and anger.

So I decided to play out a new form of revenge…

Not old-school revenge…you know, slash his tires, visit-his-girlfriend-at-the-office or take out billboard signs saying what a jerk he is.

That is so passé.

I'm talking of a new-style of revenge… the kind where you focus on living your greatest life. I remembered the dignity and poise that Vanessa Williams displayed when she was de-throned as Miss America for scandalous photos taken in her youth. She retreated, discovered a new reservoir of personal power, re-invented, and is now recognized as an accomplished singer, a respected actor and all the while placed high priority on being an engaged mother. Now that is sweet revenge. Living your greatest dreams.

The revenge fantasies I would host were all variations of me being a fun, spiritually connected mom raising smart, active, connected, happy and big-hearted kids; becoming ultra successful at my writing and speaking career; having money to satisfy my needs, wants, charities and whimsical escapades; and being cherished by an amazing, successful man who adores my children and me.

The standard revenge fantasy that I play at red lights (when I should be kegeling) is one of me being in pure contentment, laughing as the children and I are playing frisbee on the beach with my sexy, enlightened man. He looks at me with devouring eyes and, in a flash, returns to being playful with the children.

Let me rest with that image for a moment... ahhh...

I always thought revenge was a bad thing... but this new style of revenge was invigorating. I figured I'd do whatever it took for me to move out of the clingy, desperate-woman mode, even if it meant escaping into fantasy.

I noticed that if I pretended that my revenge fantasy was actually true, something changed in me...

My posture became better... my face would glow... I would have more sass and expression in my communication... and I would be more patient and more fun loving with the kids.

That is the kind of revenge that I want. Even if it was an illusion, so too was what I had been living.

Live well, it's the best revenge.

- The Talmud -

37

One day, while driving I was feeling a terrible hollow in my stomach and I prayed for a healing. I kept visioning circles of women around me supporting me.

That same evening, there was a message on my voicemail from Val, one of the moms at the kids' school, inviting me to join her Artist's Way group.

A window had opened.

The group was already in their fourth session and they graciously opened their hearts to me. This circle of women so beautifully collected together were all healers—by trade or by simply being who they are. This became a place where I could let go and know I had somewhere safe to land.

Working through Julia Cameron's book proved to be both revealing and cleansing. The simple strategy of journaling, weekly exercises and sharing discoveries in a trusted circle helped me to see the beauty and the artistic possibility in all that I was experiencing.

Some months prior I had taken a course called The Mastery of Self Expression—which helped me shed my attachment to image—and our ongoing meetings surprisingly had all the men in that group dropped off for legitimate reasons. My group now consisted of six solid, open, vulnerable, dynamic women. Yet another women's circle for me to rest in or get some whoop ass… whichever would be in my highest interest at the time.

Living From Truth, another incredible program with ongoing group practices, also surprisingly became organically free of men. Men would eventually enter my space, but for now, healing was to happen with my circles of sisters.

My long-time friends tried awkwardly to support me. But as I was changing, the easiest people to explore the change with were people who were also morphing into their new lives. Here, I wasn't confined to old images of me—I could be whoever I wanted to be, and explore the many aspects of me that had lain dormant for so long.

38

Sometimes I couldn't see the forest for the trees and felt completely without support.

I had many close friends, but for some reason, I couldn't think of them when I was in a state of "aloneness." And when I asked a casual acquaintance to be my "In Case of Emergency" contact person, all I could remember was deep shame that I had nowhere else to turn.

I'm not sure why that was the overriding emotion. But it was.

The truth is, I would never hesitate calling my children's father in case of emergency; we are still family.

And I did.

He followed the ambulance as they took me to the hospital with suspected kidney stones. He stayed with me until the doctor discharged me. I toggled between feeling fraudulent as we pretended we were still married so he could act as my representative, feeling aware of my aloneness, and then being so thankful that he was there.

They discharged me with a healthy supply of Percocet and relaxants and he took the children to his place while I dosed up and waited for the stone to pass.

Finally, it passed.

It was miraculous. There was instant relief and I was back being me with not a single remnant of the torture I had endured over the past twelve excruciating hours.

I looked at the sieve that caught the stone that had leveled me.

I have extremely high pain threshold so surely this must have been close to the size of a boulder that had lodged itself in my urinary tract. I was humbled when I realized that I had been knocked down to my knees by a tiny grain of sand. I had to laugh.

The pain level had been equivalent to hard labor and there was no great prize at the end. At least, it makes sense to be in agony for an eight-pound baby—but for a grain of sand?

I laughed in awe at the omnipotence of a grain of sand—enough to knock out "super mom!"

I believe every physical ailment correlates to an emotional one. According to medical doctors, kidney stones are the result of poor diet and dehydration.

Louise Hay, with her knowledge of the emotional body, says kidney stones are lumps of unresolved anger. No surprise with either diagnosis for me.

By the way, my mother, brothers and nephew jumped in the car and drove 12 hours to see me when they heard of my kidney stone. How could I have ever thought I was all alone?

39

The truth shall set you free. But first, it will piss you off.

- Gloria Steinem -

What the hell is the truth?

I don't just mean that philosophically, but seriously, what is it?

I mean, everything I lived was a sham wasn't it?

Now with all my vision boards and affirmations, haven't I now just traded up in my illusions?

As I read some of the popular self-help books and began to learn more, the more evident it became:

I am the truth.

My beliefs are my truth and my life is evidence of it.

Whatever I truly believed would happen, actually happened.

That sucks.

No one to blame.

So, if there is no one else to blame, then my life is what it is because I never expected it to be any different.

I said OK to this? Come on, seriously?

I struggled with this concept. All the crap in my life had been created by me?

I did not like the sound of that... I tried to hide from it, deflect it, put the blame on others, but the truth became pretty evident. The struggle to fight the obvious was becoming increasingly tiresome.

I create my reality.

Well, there was nothing about that theory I liked except that, if I changed my thoughts and beliefs, then, presumably, things in my life would change as well.

So, in earnest, I began to examine my thoughts and beliefs.

40

I tried hard to keep money talk at bay—not just to the children, but to myself as well. I hated facing the reality of the situation and confronting the truth about my own careless spending. Meticulous accounting was not my style.

Any accounting for that matter.

As a principle of good parenting, I was already adept at saying "no" to many of the nonsense requests, but as money became scarcer, the no's became more frequent. Their jobs as little kids is to badger until someone breaks down. Their dad was far more generous with their requests than I was. I was torn up inside by having to deny their requests. I tried to shield them from the stress of it all, but my fear around the lack of money was paramount.

One day we left their dentist's office with a staggeringly large bill. Overwhelmed with fear, I sat in the van in the parking lot with the three children and wept.

They were silent.

The cat was out of the bag.

We were poor.

41

I felt like crap every time I had to say to the kids, "We can't afford it." I hated the sound of that. I flipped back and forth… sometimes I felt so financially abundant when practicing the art of manifestation, and then with a thud I would become frozen with fear thinking about the credit card bill.

The necessary expenses were barely manageable, but it was the ongoing barrage of requests for toys and eating out that choked me.

The continuous assault on the house made for more expenses. I had seen other people's homes, and I knew that, by comparison, I was raising chimpanzees.

There were daily additions of new stains on the carpets, there were broken windows and mirrors from sporting upsets, then there were broken curtain rods from hanging on the curtains, and there were damages to the floor by a certain curious monkey who just "had to know" what was under the linoleum.

I was not amused.

My fear around our lack of money became part of the air we breathed.

I am a believer in the law of attraction and when I was conscious of what I was creating, I could see its potency. However, deep in my psyche, I did not believe that I could manifest money.

One day during one of our back scratch talks—my son loves me to scratch his back at night and it is here that we share golden moments of private, real communication—he asked me if we were poor.

I was silent as I thought about it and then I said, "No, we are not poor. We never have been poor. We are wealthy in many ways. In fact, I think we are the wealthiest people we know."

He said, "Yeah, yeah, I know THAT, but are we poor in money?"

I replied, "No. I was poor in my attitude and my belief, but that will change right now. We are not poor, we never were and I am sorry that I ever let you think that."

42

But changing was not that simple.

I remember telling them once that I was going to treat them to soft-serve ice cream cones and when we got to the order window they all changed their minds and begged for the whipped frozen treats that cost four times the price of the cones that I had originally agreed to buy.

I, overwhelmed with their requests, shouted at them in the drive thru for being so ungrateful. Not a stellar parenting moment that is for sure.

Since then, they still ask for what they want but when I say, "It is difficult for me to say no but I need to, and I need you to understand that," they give me a supportive look and let go of their requests.

I don't know how many mixed signals I am giving them about money. Ask and you shall receive. Don't ask. We are rich. We are poor. Sigh… the contradictions…

43

How are we financially going to make it? I was nauseous with worry.

We have to sell the house and clear the debt.

Where will we live? How did we get into so much debt?

I really want to feel abundance and trust, but I was riddled with fear and worry.

I prayed for a miracle.

I had been on a waiting list for over two years to join a community kitchen, but since cooking facilities were scarce, no new groups were being formed. It was miraculous timing that in conversation with one of the neighborhood moms, she asked if I wanted to join her church group's community kitchen!

Once a month we met at a cooking facility and chopped, stirred, grated and created meals for our families—enough meals to last for half the month. It was an exhausting day, but the camaraderie of being with women in community, all working together, was such an enlivening event. The meals were inexpensive and the experience was rich.

A surprise side benefit was that we had access to the overstock after the local food banks and other agencies had collected their share. I took home pantry items and fresh foods and shared them with the children's father and other families that I knew.

I silenced the inner voices of shame that wanted to be heard. I concentrated on being grateful for the abundance that was being offered to me.

One morning when I was going to pick up some food from the overstock warehouse, I reflected on the irony that just before leaving the house I had given a donation to a worthy charity and here I was, only 15 minutes later, receiving charity.

I understood in that moment that this is what wealth is intended to be:

To give AND to receive.

It's all about flow, Baby!

Slowly, I became more adept at releasing my money fears and becoming more observant as to how I was already being taken care of.

44

We went to three different mediators. We were not necessarily in conflict. Oh sure, there were areas of contention, but we were not at odds with each other.

We were both avoiders and our time lapses and lazy stalemates forced us to get a new mediator. There was one jewel that was worth the extraordinary fee that the second mediator charged: At our first meeting she said:

"We do not treat children like victims of divorce. We believe that they chose you as parents knowing that you would get divorced."

That was a real departure from the guilt-laden approach I had been taking.

Instantaneously, I was relieved and began to see our children as powerful, knowing individuals versus the sad, broken victims that I had been making them out to be.

Surely, if I continued to see them as victims, then they would assume victimhood as their mantra. But if I adopted the notion that they were masterful creators who chose to experience this with us, then all guilt and shame disappeared.

Now, free from those weighted thoughts, we could fully engage in this experience together.

For a long while, we just continued our normal roles. I would be with the children for 95 percent of the time and he showed up for the parts that he liked. Because this was normal for us, it continued to be our way.

So when the mediators suggested that he start taking the children for over-night visits and weekends, I just about threw up. Fear ran rampant in my body. He looked nervous at the idea, but he also knew that this had hit a nerve with me.

He capitalized on that for a couple of months. He began threatening to take them for half of the time and I froze. I knew he didn't want fifty-fifty. What he wanted was something to hold as power over me. And when he found out it wouldn't greatly alter his financial commitments, he quickly retreated from his position. I just held my breath during that time, entirely unsure on how to proceed.

46

Shortly after the mediator recommended that the children begin overnight visits with their father, I was visiting my family and having a much-needed talk with my stepfather.

Nurdin listened to me as I poured out all the reasons why I thought it wasn't in the best interest for the children to be with their father. After all, who would look after them?

After listening to me splutter through my tears, Nurdin simply said: "Farhana, you are under the mistaken belief that you are the one taking care of these children."

I was shocked at that statement, but knew it was profound. I closed my eyes and breathed the statement in. As I sat in silence breathing this message in, I had a vision.

It was of Prophet Abraham, taking his son for sacrifice, heeding the message from God. And at the moment of sacrifice, God replaced his son with a lamb. And then I heard the clearest voice booming between my ears saying, "Trust Me."

Peace entered my constricted body and a smile came over my teary and make-up soiled face, and I knew that I need not worry about my children. God has them perfectly taken care of.

What really saddened me was to see how language had suddenly changed about the homes. Now it was "Mom's place" or "Dad's place." Home was no longer theirs.

I felt like a pot of stirring emotions. I was reluctant to let the children go yet thankful for the moments to be alone.

When he would pick them up, I felt a bit of vengeance, hoping that he would finally have a taste of what raising the children was all about. In the beginning, I still made their lunches and helped them with their homework on his days with them, but eventually he shifted into those responsibilities as well.

I noticed that if I let it go and the ball dropped, it wasn't irreparable and he was a pretty fast study.

In fact, every six months it seemed that he shifted into a new connectedness of being a parent. He seemed to enjoy them more and they began to trust being around him more. I told him that I noticed it and I was happy for all of them. I admitted to him that a piece of me enjoyed being the "go to" parent and I was envious about sharing that space. He chuckled and said I was still, and forever would be, the "go to" parent. That was kind of him to say.

48

My son called me at 5:22 in the morning from his dad's place. He had a bad dream. He dreamt that his dad and the other woman were getting married.

I comforted him by telling him that dreams are not reality, they are simply our fears that are expressing themselves.

He spluttered out, "I hate her."

I asked, "Do you think she was the reason Dad and I split up?"

He screeched a painful, "Yes."

"Son, she is not the reason we broke up. Dad and I had been over for a long time."

I continued. "I don't have a say on who Dad dates, but if I did, I would pick her."

"You would?" he asked incredulously.

"Yes, because she is a good mother and she already loves my kids. What more could I want than someone who loves my children?"

He seemed to rest a little easier. And while I would have many more talks with the two older children, it pretty much followed the same style. Each time I told them that they were free to love her as well and it did not constitute a betrayal to me, I could feel their relief.

49

I did want them to be free to love anyone without feelings of betrayal, but that didn't mean I didn't have my own painful moments.

I twinged at the thought of my daughters becoming best friends with "her." I wondered whom they would talk to about their problems, their crushes, and their dreams. I wondered whom they would be with when they each got their first period. Who would be the one to usher them through the initiation into womanhood?

I ached when I thought of someone else being that person in their lives.

The daughters that I looked forward to experiencing these things with may ultimately share those experiences with another woman of influence and importance.

50

On the first New Year's Eve after we separated, the children and I went to a family party organized by a group that I have done much of my spiritual growth work with. There was a spontaneous dyad where people partner up and the Master Trainer was going to give an instruction for the pair to complete.

My oldest daughter, now six-years old, was hanging out with me at the time and we excitedly became partners.

Then, we received our instructions. The Master Trainer said, "Look into your partner's eyes in silence and feel the pain that they have endured this year."

Oh my goodness... I looked into her eyes and saw for the first time the depth of pain that she never verbally expressed. She did not tear. She held herself in perfect posture as I explored the depth of her soul in silence. I felt oneness with her pain. It was poignant and heartbreakingly beautiful to "get" her and "see" her.

She gave me a spontaneous kiss and wrapped her arms around me. Then, suddenly free of the unspoken burden of grief she had been carrying; she skipped off to join the other children.

I was thankful she left… there was no need for her to bear the weight of witnessing my pain.

51

My son has probably had the most cycles in his healing process. He is fiercely loyal to both of us and takes on a tremendous amount of personal responsibility to ensure we are both being treated fairly by one another.

He was the one who struggled the most with his dad having a girlfriend. For him, it amounted to even less time with his dad. And he so desperately wanted male company and role modeling. He struggles to understand his place in his dad's relationships and at the same time would hold deep concern for my well-being.

He is not yet a man, but feels he must play that role in the house.

One morning, we had a fight about something or another. Breakfast was on the table, but he was not to be found. I looked around the house and growing fear started to build up in my chest. I opened the front door and there he was—shoveling the snow from our first blizzard of the season.

I am troubled by the self-appointed responsibility that he bears on his shoulders, and yet feel honored and proud of the chivalrous young man that he is.

52

One of my sons" most pronounced cycles was when he declared a boycott on fun.

Fun became a loyalty issue for him. If he was having fun with me, he felt he was betraying his dad. And despite his dad's best efforts to engage him and be playful with him, he remained loyal to each of us through his sullenness.

I decided to do something to shake us out of the constricted life we seemed to be living. On my son's Lifeboard was Disneyland. I would take them to Disneyland!

I didn't exactly know how, but with my laser-focus vision on making it happen, things started to fall into place. That autumn, my sister-friend Cristina and I took the two older children to Disneyland. It was, after all, the "happiest place on earth" and I could think of nothing more that I wanted to be able to give to these children.

The moment the plane started to move on the tarmac, my son announced he didn't want to go and then proceeded to hold us hostage for the entire trip with his I–told–you–I–didn't–want–to–come foul attitude. I whipped into the after–all–that–I–have–done–for–you type of parent, having created this opportunity against all odds.

It felt like so long since we had laughed. I just wanted us to be burden free for a few days.

Within four minutes of entering into the gates of the "happiest place on earth," he said that he was bored and wanted to go home. I was beaten. I was battling a painful sinus infection and that, coupled with my son's boycott on fun, became too much for me. I started to cry.

And then I ordered him to have fun.

My perception on how we would feel at the "happiest place on earth', was not meeting with reality at all.

My daughter, on the other hand, thankfully enjoyed herself. Thank goodness Aunty Cristina was there to ensure her experience was a success and to make sure that, in my frustration, I didn't leave my son behind.

53

As I fumbled my way around single parenting to my three children, I toggled between being present and totally engaged with them to being in complete preoccupation with my thoughts.

Since my commitment to be observant about my thoughts, I became enormously interested in what I was thinking and how I was acting and reacting through life's various circumstances. It was like I was meeting myself for the first time and was curious to find out more about what made me tick.

Because I was in observation and not in judgment, I began to see how much I actually lied. Almost everything I conveyed was not the truth.

I had never really checked in with myself before to know that. I did what I thought people wanted, or what I thought I wanted, and, unknowingly, was completely out of touch with my truth.

It wasn't so much that I had difficulty telling the truth, I just had difficulty knowing what it was.

If I paused for only a moment to inquire within what I wanted to do, or what I thought of a situation, it was almost always different from what my knee jerk response had been. I had become so out of touch with "my truth" that to discover it was like finding a cache of personal power.

Then, in one of my courses, I had a breakthrough discovery: the tremendous power of declaring truth out loud to someone.

In partners, we took turns responding to the question posed by the Master Trainer. The responses were often surprising and revealing because we were challenging ourselves to speak the hidden truth. You know, the part that we usually keep separate from one another in an effort to "look good."

It was here that when I claimed my "uglies," the shifts began to occur.

I dissolved my need to be right, look good, be profound or be funny.

I was none of those things.

I was just real.

I made no effort to sanitize myself.

It felt like I had hundreds of blockages and every time I had the courage to declare the truth about something... my shame about my parenting, my closet smoking, my sexual shame, my fears about success, my anger at playing small, my judgments about others and a hundred more revelations—those blockages began to spontaneously dismantle.

Nobody offered advice.

None was needed.

We all know everything we need to know.

Truth is the panacea.

And like some medicine, while it may sting when applied—it's designed properties are always to clean, heal and make whole again.

Yes. Glorious Truth. You are to be worshipped.

That which is within you and expressed will set you free.
That which is within you and not expressed will eat you
on the inside.

- Gospel of Thomas -

54

I meditated.

The act of doing something for me, and something that was calm after all the chaos that surrounded me, was a relief to escape into.

My need for some quiet time to journal or just listen to my own meandering thoughts became increasingly necessary.

It was like food and water.

Sustenance, in order to become the person I wanted to be.

Every waking hour (and many sleeping hours) was spent in some form of contemplation. In my contemplations and my own flowering curiosity, I noticed a shift.

As long as I was engaged in my own thoughts, I spent less and less time thinking about what he was thinking.

I became less interested in others" opinions about me and more curious of what I thought of myself.

Slowly, the person whose opinion became most important to me was... Me!

In my curiosity, I asked myself, "Where am I one-hundred percent responsible for the breakdown of my marriage?"

I would ask that question in the quiet morning hours and a fleeting thought would come up and I would marinate in it and discover that, yes, I was one-hundred percent responsible for that piece. And that piece... oh yes, and that one too... geez!

At first, I had resisted the notion of taking one-hundred percent responsibility. But, as long as I resisted, I was still blaming him and I was not free.

By me claiming my one-hundred percent, didn't mean that he didn't have his own one-hundred percent.

We are all one-hundred percent responsible for the lives we have created.

Whenever I uncovered where I contributed to the breakdown of the marriage, I would call him to apologize and own my piece.

He is a good-natured man so he always accepted my apology, chuckled at my insights and told me I think too much. But I always waited for something. I quietly waited for HIM to apologize.

He never did.

I had an epiphany one day.

I understood why he HAD to leave me.

I realized that I was forever fixing and not allowing natural consequences and experiences to occur.

I was in the way.

I was so busy trying to direct his life that I spent little time directing mine.

I was in the way.

He HAD to leave me in order to experience his own life.

I told him what I discovered and he graciously accepted my insight and apology. When I hung up, something felt different... I wondered what it was.

Then I realized that I was no longer waiting for him to apologize.

I was now FREE.

> Emancipate yourselves from mental slavery,
> none but ourselves can free our mind.
>
> *- Bob Marley -*

56

But, it was hard to release being right. I mean, I LIKE being right. I didn't want to be hostage to the anger that was leeching into me, so I needed to put some of my personal development training to use. Direct from Dale Carnegie's Golden Rule book:

Rule #17: Try honestly to see things from the other person's point of view.

Hmmm... Worth a shot.

He meets a girl who looks past his history and just enjoys him. She laughs a lot, is bright eyed with big dreams, and accepts him and adores him for who he is. They marry a short time later and just like that, she changes.

She goes from fun loving to proper. From accepting to judgmental. From nurturing to selfish. From nymphomaniac to frigid.

She becomes the polar opposite to what he knew.

He feels duped. Lied to. Cheated. Married. Committed. Stuck.

He is a loyal sort who makes the best out of all situations so he tries his best to fit in and conform. Meanwhile, while he adapts, he also loses himself. She is a good daughter-in-law and a good sister-in-law, but she is not necessarily a good wife anymore. She is sexually un-available and constantly sculpting him into a "better him."

They have their first child. She turns more neurotic trying to keep up with appearances and creating a façade of a picture perfect life and he feels the irreparable divide widening between him and his wife.

He now carries the weight and burden of providing financial stability to his family. She used to be the primary income earner and now she seems content to shift all financial responsibility to him. He feels the pressure.

A second child is born. He feels more pressure and even less connec-tion. She doesn't even speak to him anymore. Not really. She barks out orders, but that is it. She has become demanding and unappreciative with a never-ending "to do" list.

They are stuck.

She wants to take courses. They cost a lot of money. But he wants her happiness so he agrees. When she returns home from a course, he doesn't know who will be coming home. A loving woman, a warrior woman, or another version of "fix him" woman.

He *takes some of the programs his wife suggests. He certainly feels the benefits—mostly seeing her happy again. She is fun to connect with. But, it all feels like it takes a lot of effort. What is the point?*

Remember when they did things effortlessly? These courses make her vulnerable and make her cry uncontrollably sometimes. It seems like a lot of effort to have fun again.

And she always wants more. She is never satisfied.

A third child is born. They are more disconnected than ever. He wants to do the right thing, but he is dying within. He douses his pain with beer and finds emotional comfort in an uncomplicated woman.

What to do?

Let her know that he is exiting the relationship. He is not leaving the children's lives, but he can no longer find happiness with her.

She is just not a happy person anymore. She is in too much personal pain and he can't help her.

He wants his own happiness... with another woman. This other woman is different... she laughs all the time and doesn't seem eternally unhappy or disappointed with him. She is easy to fall in love with.

So, as his wife suspects another woman, he neither confirms nor denies, trying to ease her into the notion of the possibility. He doesn't know another way that would be less painful... for him.

He does not like confrontation.

He just wants out. And he doesn't want to cause injury to anyone. Not to his kids and not to his wife, but he knows for sure he can no longer be in this marriage.

Then, on Valentine's Day, she gives him an out...

57

The summer after our marriage ended, I took yet another self-development course, which gave me a new angle to view my role in the deterioration of our marriage.

The assignment this time was to truly own the place where I was responsible for the failure of my marriage and tell him so. So yet again, I made another "clean up on aisle 9" call to him and said:

> "There are so many areas of my life that I am uncovering that are unauthentic and rooted in protecting an image that I have of myself. I am shocked at the lie of a life I have led until now.
>
> I apologize for the times that others saw a supportive wife and you saw a critical one.
>
> I realize now that I put far more effort into the eventual breakup than I put into the relationship. I had already visualized the style in which I would conduct myself when you left.
>
> I had truthfully only prepared for one outcome. I realize now, that at a deep level, I have always believed myself to be unlovable and that "happily ever after," as engraved on our wedding rings, did not seem like a possibility for me.
>
> I am sorry for my need to be right and my subtle criticisms.
>
> I am sorry for my need to look good and to make you look bad."

He brilliantly said, "Umm... Thanks... you know, this was my fault too."

I have to give this to him: He has never made me feel badly about the type of wife I was. He has never criticized me or held me responsible or blamed me in any way for the breakdown of our marriage.

Declaring my responsibility to him was as much a gift to him as it was to me.

58

The baby was a little over a year old when we parted and knew of no other way of life. However, she kept insisting that her dad and I hug and kiss.

She even started telling me that "Daddy loves you" and was starting to tell him the same thing about me. It surprised me, but I suppose she was just trying to reconcile the images that she was seeing in the media about other families being together.

For a while her favorite thing to watch was our wedding video. We had never even watched our wedding video before but her fascination with it was really interesting.

I looked at us in the video and saw how young and hopeful we were… it was nice to see that look of unjaded love.

One day I spent the entire day organizing photos and found myself sad and unsettled. I could see how fast the children were growing, and I thought of how I have forced them to grow up because of my impatience.

I saw pictures of their dad and remembered how young and playful he used to be. I always thought that I carried all the stress of parenting, but when I look at the way we had changed from the photos I see that he, too, carried some of the responsibility.

And, on a side note, I noticed that I had a nice figure, but I had always been so wrapped up on thinking that I was fat that I didn't notice that I was OK. Now I would be happy with the figure that I had back then. Dang! Why didn't I know?

59

While his commitment to the marriage dissolved, bill collectors were a little more insistent on him honoring his commitments to them.

Nine months after we separated, phone calls and overdue notices started coming in from suppliers associated with his business. I had not been involved in his business affairs for many months, so I was shocked to learn of the staggering debt his business had accumulated since our separation.

True, running two households on the same income was difficult. Perhaps twenty-five percent of the debt accumulated could be assigned to running two households, but what about the rest?

We never had any discussion around this—not particularly hard for two avoiders. I was very clear (to myself anyway) that aside from the incremental expenses from running two households, the rest was not my debt. Therefore, I did not want to energetically assume any of the responsibility for it.

Legally however, we were still a couple and I would be held financially liable as well.

I held the intention of him being an honorable man and that he would do the right thing. Every morning, I held him in meditation with an open heart as being an honorable man. In this, I started feeling profound waves of love and respect for him because I could already feel him being that.

A couple of weeks later, the mediator called to say that my husband had contacted her and that I was not to assume any of that debt and that he was to be fully responsible for it. She was stunned. I was not... he was the honorable man that I had envisioned him to be.

60

I worry about him. I cannot seem to detach from wanting to be his caretaker.

It's not that I want to be, I just am.

I worry about the choices he makes and I can feel a dark cloud hanging over him all the time.

I had an instinctive feeling about the wonderful life that I knew lay ahead of me, and felt tremendous guilt at leaving him behind. The fact that it was he who left me was irrelevant.

And then I thought, "If I knew I didn't have to worry about me because I knew that the Universe will look after me, why should I worry about him?"

Won't the Universe look after him too?

I began to see that it was arrogant of me to feel worried for him.

Just as God's got my back, so too does God have his.

61

One evening their dad was already at the house ready to watch the children when Deb, my shamanic-healer friend, came by to pick me up for a meditation circle. She told me the energy between him and me is so clean that she wouldn't have known we were apart.

It really is very clean. We don't entertain a life together. We are happier apart.

Even when we are together, when his parents visit or at an event for the children, there is no strain. He is not the kind of person who likes confrontation and generally likes to get along with everyone, so, he makes friendship easy.

Prior to our break-up, I had booked a phone session with a marriage coach. Her only availability at that time was February 15—one day after our fated Valentine's Day.

When she called, I was in no state to talk... or listen. After all, my marriage had ended the day before and the last thing I needed at that point was a marriage coach.

She said something though that remained with me.

She said, "There may be more truth in you being apart than in you being together."

I think she was right. I know she was right.

On the first anniversary of our break-up, I silently thanked him for leaving me.

62

As a child I would talk to God often. I don't know why I ever stopped. I always felt connected with God, and during this time of change I was ready to resume conversation.

In the yoga position of child's pose, I asked God:

What do you want to tell me about being your Divine Child?

You are perfect in all your attempts. You are no different than the baby. There is no concern whether she will "get it" or not. It is joyful to watch her learn; to observe her tenacity. The same is so for you.

Through your own discoveries, bumps and, yes, even through your frustrations, I am entertained in joy and in total confidence that you will indeed "get it."

See no difference between the baby and yourself. See no difference between you and Me. Keep exploring... it is all waiting for you.

63

On the following Mother's Day my son brought me eggs and toast and served me in bed. I wondered how that could happen when he wasn't allowed to touch the stove. Then I heard the garage door close and I realized that his dad drove thirty minutes to make me breakfast as my son had requested of him, and then he drove back. I was so touched by both of these men.

But still, all day I felt jittery... My son and her son were on the same baseball team and we were all going to be at the game that afternoon. It would be hard to pretend that we did not notice each other.

I had an unexpected bolt of pain when I saw their vehicles parked side–by-side. It was the first time we would all be together at an event. My anxious nervousness started triggering heart palpitations. I knew I was off kilter. My son ran out to join his team and the girls and I stayed in the van for a few more minutes while I took some deep breaths and prayed for peace and calm.

As we walked to the ball diamond, my youngest daughter, now two-and-a-half years old, so full of love, spotted the "other woman" and promptly slid down my body and ran towards her.

I didn't hold her into me tighter by even one degree.

She was free to go.

I didn't energetically hold her back.

She was free to love.

And in that moment, when pain and love were both in full presence, I expanded my heart and pushed my little girl forth energetically with more love.

From the corner of my eye, I was aware that our eldest daughter, now six years old, was attentively watching me and keenly observing everything.

Later she was feeling cold and wanted to sit down. I wrapped her in a blanket and told her to go and sit on the other woman's lap, as she was seated on a chair.

My daughter looked deep into my eyes to assess whether this was in fact OK. I assured her it was, and off she went.

I have known from the beginning that my youngest child was a gift for the world. She belonged to everyone. So open and so loving. My older daughter however was MY girl. She is my twin soul.

I could feel the pain grip my chest and throat. But I invited love to take over my feelings and almost instantly the pain subsided.

In that one moment, I set us all free and open to love whomever we wanted to.

Love has no loyalty.

I was amazed that the moment I chose love, it seemed to dissolve the pain.

In fact, I surprisingly felt no pain.

It was miraculous.

64

A few days later, as I reflected, I realized that on this Mother's Day I got to "walk my talk."

In my mind's eye, I was able to live into being the grandest vision of me that I had held.

THAT was my Mother's Day present.

I now understand that contradictory feelings—both love and fear— can be in place at the same time.

It is not the absence of one feeling that makes the choice. It is in the choosing that the choice is made.

When I struggle between fear and courage and I choose courage, fear dissolves.

The moment that I choose love over pain, pain dissolves.

I choose love.

Note: Apparently, on that Mother's Day, they were no longer together and he had a new girlfriend. I did not know this. I asked myself if that lessened the impact of that experience and I decided it did not. I was operating by the variables I thought were in place. And, love was, and still is, the answer.

Third Stage

Once brought to the surface, and kissed by the light, the lotus blossoms...

We must let go of the life we have planned so as to
have the life that is waiting for us.
- Joseph Campbell -

65

Their dad's Blackberry met with the river and thinking that it was non redeemable, he gave it to the kids. For days it was the coveted toy.

One night when tucking my son in bed, I heard a clear voice in my head instructing me to look at the Blackberry.

I fixed a cup of tea and sat with the Blackberry in hand and much to my surprise, all the text messages were still intact. I wasn't a particularly curious sort that way because every piece of information I uncovered just caused me more torment so I usually stayed away from being an investigative reporter.

But, since the voice in my head TOLD me to look, I flipped through his texts with his new girlfriend and marveled at their creative use of text messages. It was undeniably more colorful than the functional "pick up milk" texts I used to send. I felt I needed a cigarette after reading some of the sexy exchange.

And then I read his correspondence with a different woman... and then another...and I began laughing uncontrollably. I didn't know why I was laughing but I was on the ground rolling around in laughter.

I can't recall a time where I laughed that hard. It was such a strange reaction. I mean, there was no part of me that wished anything ill on any of them so I really did not understand my reaction.

I giggled all the way to bed that night, still confused at my bizarre reaction.

After a couple of very giddy days, I was on the phone with my mother and telling her the story, I was very giggly and had a hard time getting the story out. She even asked me if I was drunk. I said no, and then with laser beam clarity, I got it.

All this time, I thought it was ME.

I thought I wasn't good enough. I thought I wasn't desirable enough. I thought I just simply wasn't enough.

The truth was, him being with other women had nothing to do with me. That was all about him.

With the weight of "not being enough" being lifted off my shoulders and the veil of inadequacy instantly vaporizing, I experienced levity that showed up as a three-day laughing gas stint.

This was much more enjoyable than the other "gas" stint.

66

My son advises me that dad's new girlfriend is moving in. Huh?

I didn't realize that she was a serious girlfriend as he had claimed that she was just a friend. And now she was moving in? Well, that just flies in the face of every agreement we had about how the children would be introduced to any significant other. I was not impressed.

I called him. He said, "Yes, she and her son are moving in."

I am furious at his cowardice. Why couldn't he tell me instead of having the children once again be the ones to relay the news.

I asked to meet her—after all, she would be co-parenting my children—but they are both edgy and combative. I wasn't sure what to make of it. I had always been friendly with his girlfriends. My theory was that I had better get into good relationship with his girlfriends because they were persons of influence with my children.

Over the next few months the tension eased between us and we were able to have civil small talk but I noticed she behaved differently towards me than his previous two girlfriends had done.

Then, a couple of weeks after the Blackberry texts incident, I went back to re-read the texts in hopes of receiving another dose of crazy laughter, but this time, I was able to comprehend more of what the other messages meant.

Including that this new girlfriend had actually been with him for years... and the son she had was their son.

Asshole.

67

The information that I pieced together threw me for a loop and I entered into a new cycle of processing what the hell was going on for me.

Day 1: I was calm. Actually, the more accurate statement would be catatonic.

Day 2: The thaw came over my frozen state and made way for a pain that took me by surprise in its velocity. I bawled like a baby and rocked myself back and forth as I tried to make sense of the huge web of lies. Every single part of the marriage felt like it had been a lie. What was real? I didn't know.

I was surprised at my emotional reaction. I had no lingering thoughts of wanting to be with him but the pain of betrayal was so deep. With the further crumbling of everything that I had been able to salvage as "good" in our marriage, I felt like I had to re-arrange my brain in every way. I fell asleep thoroughly exhausted.

Day 3: I was angry. Livid. Luckily the kids were away for the week-end so I could scream expletives at random throughout my day.

But the kicker was… I was scheduled to give a radio interview on how to have a loving divorce. How could I be authentic when all I really felt like was throttling the bastard?

I took a shower and as I let the water run over me, I spoke angrily to God. "Well, you obviously decided that now was good timing for me to find all this out—just as I head into the interview! I don't feel like I have anything to say, so I tell you what God, YOU do the talking."

As the water streamed down my head, I visualized my mind being hollow and completely open, my body becoming a vessel for light. I went into the interview with nothing to say—no script, no notes, nothing.

And what was said was beautiful. It was real, honest and inspirational. I was being inspired in real time with the words God was choosing to come out of my mouth.

When I completed the interview, I understood then that I was completely supported with all the wisdom it would take to see me through to a magnificent, joyous life. All I had to do was empty myself so that God could take over.

68

The breaches and lies from him were more than I could handle and one day, unable to shake my anger from it all, I called a sister-friend from my car phone to help me with a much-needed state shift. While I was angry at him for his cowardice and his lies, I was also angry with myself for continuously holding out hope that something will change.

She tells me, "You are not a saint, Farhana."

"What? I'm not?" Well, that certainly changes everything!

I pulled the van over and yelled a tapestry of curses at the windshield, willing it to crack under my tirade. I spat out my fury and was further angered by the seatbelt that was keeping me trapped in place. It mirrored how I felt on the inside—I would always be trapped by him.

I loathed him.

Then, a minute later I felt done... sort of... with a note-to-self that the next time a crazed rant was required, I did not want to be trapped by an f*&%$@ seatbelt.

My whole body began to relax out of its contracted state.

Once again, I noticed that things appeared sharper and clearer, almost metaphorically helping me to see into my own life more clearly.

After driving for a few minutes, I noticed that the reel of rage was no longer running through my head. I was observing life in the present moment.

Wow, the process of getting things out was really effective...

Perhaps I should remember that when the kids are having a scream festival.

69

After the crazed-screaming-pit-stop on the highway, I knew something had shifted. It wasn't complete yet, but a shift had definitely occurred.

I realized that I was mostly mad with him for wrecking my vision of a loving divorce. I had worked hard at sainthood so that we could have a great divorce.

It's true that I wanted that for the children, but I could see now that I also wanted it for my ego.

If I couldn't be the perfect wife, I was determined to be the perfect ex-wife.

My Club Med vision for the divorce was so important to me that I allowed the lies to build up again. I told myself that peace was more important. I played the same game I always had and so did he.

I sacrificed the truth for the vision.

And now I surrender the vision for the truth.

70

I realize now that I needed to release the Club Med divorce vision. The vision was great until it wasn't great anymore.

This has freed me to allow the relationship to be whatever it is.

As long as I hold a vision clear enough on who I want to be, and leave the rest to the Divine, I cannot be disappointed.

There is nothing to hold inadequate. Everything is what it is.

I am just to concentrate on me and the life I want to have for me and my children.

I do not have the answers.

The journey is the answer and everyone's journey is his or her own.

There is no right way.

There is not just one way.

And the ways may change.

Healing, discovering, living, and learning are not linear processes.

They are cyclical.

All of life is about cycles and contradictions. I know because I am confident, aware and evolving in one minute and in a flash can feel wounded and insecure the next.

But every time I go through a cycle, my vantage point seems to be a bit different. The movement through the cycle each time seems to go a little quicker, a little smoother and I can see the gifts that came from the experience more and more easily.

And lest I get smug with my progress, every time I feel I have made big leaps in my journey, something will happen that lets me know— that as grand as my progress has been—I am only a toe-scrunch away from where I previously was.

Ahhh... the joys and pain of "the work."

Rinse and Repeat.

71

started to spontaneously wake up at 4:28 am. I was irritated by this early wakeup call. I would toss and turn until I fell asleep again.

One morning, in frustration as I was about to rustle myself into a new sleeping position, I heard this booming voice from across the room say, "WAKE UP! DON'T GO BACK TO SLEEP: THE UNIVERSE HAS SECRETS TO TELL YOU!"

I sat up, erect and quickly moved out of bed, got my robe on, went downstairs and sat. And sat. And sat. I wasn't sure what I was supposed to do or what the protocol was to receive this "message."

So I waited. At first, respectfully alert... nothing. Getting bored, I flipped through books and waited... still nothing.

Then, I picked up my journal and started writing and my pen flew with dozens of thoughts all synchronously wanting expression. I can't say where these thoughts came from, but they were wiser than my conscious mind.

So I began the practice of regular writing... some days more inspired than others... but I always noticed that I felt better after writing. Even if it was a rant, at least it was OUT and not in.

Over time, I noticed that my writing started taking on a different style. It was infused with wisdom that was beyond my day-to-day practice, but it was also consistently filled with something else.

It was filled with love and gratitude. For everyone... and for every experience.

And then I noticed...

I was filled with love and gratitude. For everyone... and for EVERY experience.

I began to see that every incident comes as a teacher. And every encounter was nourishment.

And so, I started to thank the hosts of these experiences:

I was grateful to my husband for loving me enough to set me free.

I was grateful for the other woman for being the catalyst for our break-up. I was grateful for absent friends, kidney stones, financial pressures, chaos, rejection, pain... I was grateful for it ALL because it helped me see how resilient I was.

Oh... so much gratitude... My life was filled with light.

These were the secrets of the Universe:

Nothing had been done TO me.
Everything had been done FOR me.

- Farhana Dhalla -

I am not talking about forgiveness—although it is a good goal because then I know I'm on my way to unparalleled freedom and peace.

I am talking Gratitude.

Forgiveness would imply that something was done TO me and I have now become tolerant of what happened.

Gratitude is when I recognize that what has happened has been a vehicle FOR me to grow into the person I want to be.

I realized all the gems that came to me from seemingly unsavory experiences and I understood now first-hand what God had said to Neale Donald Walsch in *Conversations with God, Book 1*: Paraphrasing here... We cannot know our light without the contrast of dark. We do not know hot without the contrast of cold and we cannot know ourselves to be love without the contrast of fear.

Every happening is a tool for us to choose love and light. It is a chance to become who we already are.

73

Once when doing an interview for a series on Empowered Women, I discovered something else... the interviewer asked me if our fateful Valentines Day was the first time I knew that he was having an affair.

I suddenly remembered a time a couple of years before the break-up when he and I were casually talking and all of a sudden I got a huge intuitive hit.

I looked at him in the eyes and said, "There is another woman. She is young with long, dark curly hair and she works at the supplier company."

He looked shocked. He fumbled his words and said there was a girl there that was sweet on him but she was way too young, I was being ridiculous. I told him that I knew he was sweet on her too. There was no emotion, no anger, nothing. I was just stating a fact.

And then we never brought it up again.

I realized while in that interview, the woman that I had the intuitive hit on was the mother of his son.

During our marriage I had focused my inquisition around the woman from Cub Scouts. All the while, there was another.

The interviewer asked me if I regretted not following up on that instinct. I sat for a moment and breathed and silently asked myself that question. And the answer was no.

In the ongoing practice of forgiving myself, I realized that I didn't hold myself in contempt anymore for not doing anything about it. I had found grace for my own fragility.

I somehow understood that everything happens in the way that it should.

And then I also realized that if I had acted on that intuitive hit, a great part of our world would have been altered. We still had one more child to bring together into this world and for that reason alone, I not only forgave myself but felt immense gratitude for my inaction.

74

With the amount of grief the finances were bringing me and the few coaching clients that were not actually bridging the financial gap, the smart and logical thing of course would be to "get a job."

Don't get me wrong, I like working. I am a hard worker, and I enjoy being in contribution, but I felt deflated every time I had to think about getting a J.O.B. I'm just not a 9-5'er anymore.

I like the world of self-employment: flex schedules to be with my kids, the time to explore myself and the freedom to lend support to others. But the cycle of feast or famine can get tiresome.

So, reluctantly, I applied for jobs.

As if the Universe agreed with my thinking, I didn't receive one phone call back. I have a pretty desirable set of transferrable skills yet I didn't get one call.

Whether it's the Universe keeping a J.O.B at bay, or my true intention of not wanting one going into effect, I couldn't tell, in either case, the calls didn't come.

I had known for a while that I needed to operate at a greater level than I had been doing. In all areas of my life I could feel the constriction of playing small.

I escaped into my meditations and started asking the Divine for advice more and more. I felt like I had been choking on the steering wheel and driving white-knuckled for a while, and I wanted a break.

I was ready to surrender to some direction.

God, tell me what I should do.

This is what I heard:

Surrender to the pen. Allow wisdom to flow through you. Know that what you receive is guided, and, even if it is your ego that is directing the communication, hold nothing there, for it too is doing its perfect job.

No need to fight or question it and keep it all separate. It is the wholeness unto which you surrender that is you. Isn't it all so interesting that you would surrender into you? That's it.

You are He/She/One/It. Surrender not only into "the good stuff." Surrender into the All—The Alpha and the Omega. Offer no friction. Be it all... the contrast is what creates. Homogeny lacks inspiration.

To inspire is to breathe. And to inspire means to create. Therefore, embrace the contrast. Out there and, in here. Enjoy. Enjoy yourself. Surrender to the joy.

I questioned the arrogance (and the credibility) of me saying that these were my communications with God. But something gorgeous happened to me along the way, somewhere in between reading my seventy-fourth personal development book and taking my twenty-ninth personal development course...

I was no longer worried about what others thought of me.

Be who you are and say what you feel because those who mind don't matter and those who matter don't mind.

- Dr Seuss -

I recognize that we are all having our communications with God, Allah, Buddha, Christ, Great Spirit, or Higher Self, all the time. We each hear a faint voice or have the feeling in our tummy that tell us the truth.

When we hesitate, we are editing the voice of Spirit.

I no longer wanted to live from my hesitation.

75

I asked God more and more about various things… from the mundane to the sublime and all the time, a voice spoke to me.

God, how can I be a better mother?

The answer was clear:
Just BE with them. PLAY with them. BE PLAYFUL.

The playfulness that had been cloaked by my seriousness had begun to peek through again and our house became vibrant and alive with a circulating door of neighborhood friends.

My children wanted my laughter again… that's what made them happy… and when I started laughing again, the laughter came more and more easily.

76

I am always comforted when I hear other children being insolent to their parents.

Inside, I breathe a sigh of relief—my kids are normal.

Or at least their kids are as messed up as mine.

There are so many scary statistics about the delinquent behavior of children from split homes that I became hyper-vigilant in observing any infraction of behavior in my children. Any back-talk or any emotional melt-down they experienced, I attributed to our "situation" and I wanted to talk about it. It turns out not everything my children did was in reaction to the separation. They were just being normal kids working out normal boundaries.

But to be sure they had safe outlets to be able to express themselves, after the separation, I enrolled the older kids in a local "Banana Splits" program. It is designed to help children talk about their feelings and navigate through their fears about parental separation.

On the last day of the program, parents were invited to watch video interviews that they had taken with the children at various times throughout the program.

Parents held their breath as they watched the medley of videos exposing their children's feelings. The pain expressed was torturous to hear, but it was necessary for us, as parents, to hear and see things from the children's points of view.

When our son was interviewed, I held half-an-inhale as his father and I watched the video together.

Our son talked of his fears about never seeing his dad again. And then his face lit up as he announced: "I have nothing to worry about. My mom and dad get along great. It's like they are best friends!"

His dad and I, both relieved, looked at each other and smiled. Yes... it was, and is, certainly worth the effort.

Now that I knew my children were thriving, it was time to address me...

77

I have always been overweight.

And I have always felt powerless to do anything about it.

It's not even like I try to do anything about it.

I am shocked when I see myself in pictures because they aren't reflective of who I feel I am.

Once, when I came home from a five-day retreat, where I had broken through emotional, mental and physical barriers, I knew that I was forever affected and changed by the experience. I felt invincible. Everything seemed within the range of possibilities.

I caught a glimpse of myself as I was passing by a mirror and I stopped in my tracks. I looked gorgeous! My face was glowing. But what really amazed me was how sexy and svelte I looked. How womanly delicious.

It astonished me that as I changed the way I saw myself in my brain, it changed the way my brain saw my body. Not a single ounce of body fat was lost, but the weight of my heavy thoughts had lifted and I saw myself in an entirely different light.

The love/hate/dismissive relationship that I had with my body still exists, but now at least I recognize that this too, is cyclical and simply a reflection of the deeper relationship I am having with myself.

I wonder if everything is just that—a reflection of our relationship with ourselves?

78

I took a hundred classes. Well, almost... on-line courses, and evening and weekend workshops were how I spent all my "free" time.

Any topic of interest to me was fair game. You name it, I took it.

My thirst for self-discovery was virtually unquenchable.

Sex, Passion and Enlightenment (a girl's gotta dream right?), writing, self expression, meditation, yoga, art, coaching, manifesting—and about a dozen courses on various energy healing modalities—are but a sampling.

There were many naysayers in my life suggesting that I was throwing my money away, but this is how I learned and this is where I healed. I listened with mild impatience to my well-intentioned family and friends and wondered if the reaction would have been the same if I went on scrapbooking "crop till you drop" weekend retreats.

I knew what I was doing brought peace for me and enabled me to be the parent I wanted to be so I continued to take courses and put into practice, as best as I could, what I was learning.

I was listening to ME.

79

Nowadays, each morning I spend a sacred hour in meditation before the rising of chaos. If I miss more than a couple of days of meditation, my equilibrium feels thrown off and the downward cycle begins.

When that occurs, the kids spot it clearly. They categorize this as "old mom."

"New mom" is way more fun to be with.

But, I wondered… Do I meditate for pleasure or for escape? Am I in freedom or in bondage? Do I HAVE to meditate in order to have some peace? Isn't that another type of bondage?

I remember a parable at the beginning of a book on Krishnamurti titled *Truth is a Pathless Land*. It was a story of a man who had his hands in handcuffs and try as he might, he could not jimmy his hands out of bondage. He asked all over town if there was anyone who could help him… no one could. He submitted to a life of bondage by these hand shackles. Then, one day he came across a blacksmith and asked whether the blacksmith could free him. The blacksmith immediately said, "Yes" and proceeded with lightening efficiency to snip the handcuffs off his hands.

The man was free! Finally free!

In gratitude to the blacksmith for releasing him, he decided to become the blacksmith's apprentice and remained in service to him for the rest of his life. He just traded in his form of bondage. From handcuffs to duty—it's all bondage.

Is my meditation bondage? Is there freedom in my meditation?

I questioned myself, if I HAD to do it in order to be peaceful, was I really free?

80

I am uncomfortable when it comes to men.

Let me clarify, at work or as a friend—no problem.

But a man showing the slightest romantic interest in me makes me want to run... fast... it's the only time the idea of jogging actually holds any appeal!

So it was no surprise that I was nervous about meeting a male colleague for coffee. I wasn't entirely sure of his intentions and became sickened with panic.

One of my sister-friends told me I needed to work through this blockage. As soon as she said the word "blockage" a light bulb went on for me.

I remembered something from Susan Jeffers" book, *Feel the Fear and Do it Anyway*. Jeffers wrote that fear is a lack of trust—not in others—but trust in our own ability to handle what comes our way.

Blockage is fear. Fear is a lie. I am truth. There is no room for blockages in my life.

I don't trust men. At least that is what I told myself. The truth was that I didn't trust myself.

In my twenties, I looked for myself in the approving eyes of others. Each time I looked to a man for validation, I lost a sense of me. I repeated this ugly cycle over and over again, my self-esteem eroding with each successive relationship.

And then I met my husband. He, in his style of complete non-judgment, temporarily salvaged me from the mental and emotional battery I had subjected myself to.

Now that I was single again, I was afraid I would return to the insecure woman I once was.

In truth, I wasn't a woman then. I was a girl who, at the time, was doing her best to try and find herself.

Now I was a woman in my forties capable of making wise decisions and good choices.

I may choose one partner, or I may not. I may choose to have different partners, or I may not. I may choose celibacy, or I may not. The point is, I can choose. I am no longer looking to be validated by another person. Nothing needs to be as it was.

I now trust me.

81

$\mathcal{S}$o, prepared to dissolve this block of fear, I met him for coffee. My instincts were correct. What was to be a business coffee with a colleague turned out to be an invitation for more.

I blurted out that I was not ready, in any way, to connect with a man right now; I had much more to learn about myself. I needed to declare that up front so that there were no mixed signals. I was hardly dignified.

He listened calmly and then said, "I am not a common man. And I do not want what a common man wants from you. I wouldn't settle for just that. You are a beautiful woman. But, you are so much more. And I would want it all. But you have made yourself perfectly clear and you are safe with me."

Geez... those were some pretty sexy words...

I was still not ready to date, but this acquaintance became a playmate, so to speak, for me to explore what it was like for me to show up one-hundred percent in truth.

I had never been truthful about what was really going on for me with a man before. He did the same. This was groundbreaking!

We had a safety agreement that there would be no intimate contact in any way. This provided me with the boundary that I needed to experience myself.

We met about five times over a three-month-period and reached such intensity in our dialogue that I discovered something quite unexpected: truth is sexy.

Our conversations were like nothing I had ever experienced before... this new level of intimacy through truthful communication restored my trust in men... and myself.

It ended without either of us saying so, but both of us knowing so. Our gift of learning from each other was complete.

82

Truth is doing phenomenal things in my life…

It is opening up my second chakra and creativity is freely flowing from me.

And, from time to time I get into the most delicious zone. It feels like I am on the brink of an orgasm twenty-four hours a day for a stretch of several days. There is no physical manipulation involved. It is an intimate, ongoing love affair with God that blisses me out and I wear the afterglow of truth as my daily attire.

The common denominators for when this happens are when I am doing a regular meditation practice and when I am experiencing breakthroughs in identifying and telling the truth. Perhaps it is the releasing of all the blocked energy.

After consulting people who could offer me insight, I learned that I was experiencing the awakening of my kundalini. From what I understand, at the base of our seat in the first chakra, is a coil of energy. When the coil of energy unravels, which can happen slowly or very quickly, it releases energy reserves that shoot up the body, through the chakras and out the crown of the head, allowing for union with the Divine.

Apparently, there are many symptoms one can have when experiencing a kundalini awakening, orgasmically (my particular favorite) is but one way.

It made me wonder if the Divine comes to me as a lover to help cleanse me of my sexual shame... to set me free and into my fullness.

For the kundalini experience alone I would highly recommend the concoction of truth and meditation.

83

It has always surprised me how quickly people whose long–term relationships have ended would begin dating immediately. I couldn't understand it. For me, it felt like there were so many things that I still needed to discover about myself and so many ways I needed to be available for my children. I couldn't figure out what their formula was.

Did they recover faster? Were they interested in knowing themselves or were they quick to find "relief?" And, is it relief at all when it is a repeat of everything that was not understood or cleared the last time around?

Or was this a way for me to escape into my head and be safe?

84

Just based on pure logistics, I wondered how I would ever be able to fit someone into my schedule. My time is so busy with the kids and I am so fully consumed with my own activities.

Having a man in my world seemed like nothing more than a distraction.

Besides... it would be too hard on the kids. After all, they had to juggle many emotional balls with their dad being in and out of relationships and I felt it my duty to ensure consistency and stability.

But it was something that was always in the back of, not only my thoughts, but my children's thoughts as well...

In the first year of my separation, the kids and I would talk about me one day having a boyfriend. And the questions were always the same..."What if we don't like him?"

My answer was always the same as well..."That's a no-brainer; I would never be with someone you didn't like. I get to date him to decide if I like him and then you guys get to decide if I should continue dating him. Besides, I totally trust your judgment."

Initially, my son would start crying at the mere notion of me possibly dating and my daughter would go Lifeboarding. She would tell me how he is really fun to hang out with, he really wants three children, he is really rich, he likes to have parties all the time, and he has a maid who cleans up after the parties. I like my daughter's style.

Eventually they stopped asking me questions about the future fictitious man.

It was all a moot topic after all; I was not dating anyone anyway.

When I decided to "surrender to the pen" as the Divine had advised me, I decided to write this book here and call it *Spiritual Divorce*. I was informed that THAT book already exists. It's by Debbie Ford. How did I not know that? I appreciate her other works, so how did her most popular book miss my radar?

As I began to write this book, my usual passion for reading had faded. Perhaps I couldn't multi-task (Can't be! I'm a woman!) or perhaps it was so I could just be engaged in my own process.

Now that I am returning to my favorite hobby of reading, I realize that particularly in the area of personal and spiritual development, nobody owns anything.

We just express. And truth does have a familiar sound to it. It is not owned by anyone. There is a collective field that we all dip into. That is why scientists in the West can make a discovery at the exact time scientists in the East do.

All those aligned to receive that information will receive it.

We are all simply pulling from the cosmos.

86

Whatever we believe we will see, we see. Quantum physics verifies that.

And I know first-hand, whatever I choose to see, I see. Sometimes that hasn't worked out so well for me...

Now, instead, I ask to be shown what I need to know.
That's it.

And then I wait. And I am shown.

I don't always know I am being shown at the time. But I'm starting to get it. I am getting tapped in, tuned in and turned on—as Abraham-Hicks would say—to the marvelous synchronicities of the Universe.

Signs come to me in so many different ways: a sister-friend may unknowingly give me a sign while she is talking about her own life, I might overhear a snippet of conversation, catch a headline, or receive an unexpected e-mail.

And sometimes it comes out of the mouths of babes...

124

87

My son and I went on a date. His idea.

He was a young prince as he opened the door for me, carried our tray and found us the perfect spot beside the fireplace.

He generously fed me his french fries, and even blew the heat off the apple pie before feeding me. I was in bliss.

Then he said to me curtly, "Stop looking at me like that!"

I asked "Like what?"

He replied "Like we are engaged!"

I chuckled. I said I couldn't help it; this was the best date I had ever been on.

And then he said, "Yeah... that's what I wanted to talk to you about. Why don't you date, Mom?"

I was taken aback and muttered quickly that I don't really get asked out on any dates. I jokingly asked him if he had any advice for me.

Much to my surprise, he role played asking me out (ain't he charming?) and when he did, the words that rolled off my tongue—like the most natural expression were:

"I'm sorry, I don't date."

We stared at each other incredulously with what I had just said and he exclaimed, "THAT'S why you don't date, Mom!"

He was right. Even if I wasn't saying the words, I was certainly giving off that energy vibe.

He said, "I need you to date, Mom. I want someone to hang out with."

I was floored. I thought he would be the one most hurt and vulnerable at the idea of me dating someone.

88

In what seemed like choreographed timing, two days later my older daughter bounced into my office to tell me about a matchmaking web site. She saw the commercial on TV and they would find me my perfect mate!

All this time I had hidden behind the nobility of giving up the notion of having a relationship so that I could be fully available for my children.

Now that this was no longer what they wanted or needed, could I really use it as my barrier?

Oh, goodness. With my excuses for keeping myself single dissolving, I asked myself, could I indeed be open to a relationship?

I started to feel panic.

I understand the Crazy Cat Lady.

Okay, follow me on this one... every couple of years or so, the news will report about a woman with far too many cats and no social life.

It didn't just happen to her suddenly. It was a slow withdrawal and shrinking of her comfort zone. No noticeable difference from day to day, just a gradual narrowing until she was mentally and emotionally deflated.

I knew now that I had to face the narrow box that I had crowded myself into. I became acutely aware of how easy it was for someone to slowly morph into the Crazy Cat Lady.

That wouldn't work for me anyway... I'm allergic to cats.

90

One day from my office I was gazing at my baby who was now growing into a bright-eyed toddler. She was watching TV in a reclined position. Suddenly, she sat up and watched something intently and a big smile came over her face. I peeked to see what it was... it was a commercial promoting a matchmaking site.

Then she ran to hug me. Sigh... Now they have all cast their vote!

So, it was time to talk to someone about relationships. I called a coach who asked me to describe the kind of relationship I wanted. After I told her, she declared:

"Oh, so you want to date Casper? Someone who is never there so you never have to be real with him?"

"Oh, I hadn't thought of it that way."

I just thought I didn't want to have to pick up his socks.

91

A year and a half after our separation, at the insistence of my sister-friends, I ventured onto an Internet dating site.

The experience surprised me on many levels. The shaky vulnerability of even declaring that I was single and open to meeting someone was scary. I also felt shame for using such a random method to attract a date.

It took tremendous courage to post a profile and with that I was rewarded with some insights.

I wrote my profile without looking at other profiles. I wrote my truth about who I was and what I was looking for. That seemed to ring authentic for many people who were trying to decipher the fiction that sometimes gets communicated on the Internet.

Every time someone asked more specifically what I was looking for in a partner, I wrote it like I was writing my wish list for the first time. It made me feel even more clear about what I was looking for and strengthened my resolve to only entertain conversation with those who were aligned in some way with that vision.

I became clear and, therefore, so did my point of attraction.

I enjoyed every piece of interaction. Even to say, "No thanks" became a joy because I knew I was choosing me and growing more confident at declaring what I wanted and what I did not.

92

A few weeks later, I arrived at the coffee shop with the children and saw their dad and our mediator at the table waiting. I quickly got the kids settled with some donuts at the neighboring table and joined their dad and the mediator to review our legal separation papers.

With little fanfare we signed the papers.

As I was signing, I thought, this doesn't change a thing. We are STILL life partners. We have children together and we will be together forever. I felt a big thud in my stomach and I didn't know whether I wanted to laugh or cry.

I felt a sinking feeling of regret; completion and yet no end; the dissolution of a dream; dissolution of an illusion. It felt too big to bear and the only person who I wanted to hug for comfort was my soon-to-be-ex-husband.

He gave me a stiff hug, which felt incomplete, he packed up the kids in his truck to whisk them to his ball game and I went off to wail in the car ride all the way to my next destination—my first blind date.

93

The date had a less than auspicious start.

I walked in with tear-smeared mascara and a trickling nose from my unexpected emotional release after having just signed the legal separation papers.

My date, very chivalrously, gave me the space to gain my composure, and filled in the conversation with his own experiences.

Sensing how fragile I still was, he took me out to dinner to celebrate my new beginning. We listened to Wayne Dyer in the car and laughed many times throughout the evening. We then completed it with a walk through the park, and star gazed in silence.

He was a gentleman who seemed to recognize that being a friend to me in that moment was the best gift he could have provided.

It was a perfect evening.

Since then, I have had a few more dates with different people…

I even dated one kind man for a couple of months but saw myself repeating old patterns of not speaking my truth nor seeing the truth and trying to make things be something other than what they were.

I was thankful for that experience and that awareness because it has made me stronger in my voice and in my intuition.

94

One day I asked God what would be the greatest gift I could give Him.

The reply was, "Your Magnificence."

This surprised me. I had always thought the greatest offering to the Divine was gratitude.

Not so.

The Divine wants our Magnificence.

I thought about it.

I would much rather my children live boldly into the fullness of their spirit than offer me thanks.

To see them in their bloom is the biggest gift I could ever conceive.

95

Now that I have relinquished my Club Med vision, I thought that perhaps it was high time I became a more active member of the "I Want it All" Club.

So, I am Lifeboarding some more... planting those powerful seeds of visualization and watching with delight and anticipation what grows.

Remember my sexy, enlightened man? Yep, he's coming... (if you happen to know him, please let me know)

My children are exploratory, creative, expressive, bright, affectionate kids. They know who they are and they are fully present to a world of infinite possibility.

They are wonderfully audacious in their Magnificence.

There is no separation between who I am and what I do.

My "being" is my work. My work is of service. And to be in service is my joy.

Abundance in all its delicious forms finds a multitude of ways to come into my life.

I submit to a life that is full of ecstatic possibilities.

96

The lotus does not apologize for its surroundings.

It blooms anyway.

Fully claiming its Magnificence.

Claim your Magnificence.

After all… what else is there to do?

Epilogue

Suffering is optional.

Suffering is a choice you make in order to fulfill and fortify your internal victim. The subtle victim deep within is always lurking about waiting for an opportunity to indulge in the self-pity that leads to suffering.

Bliss is inevitable.

No matter how exhausting, challenging or disappointing Life may feel, eventually you will return to the profound incorruptible Bliss that is your very nature. Real Bliss is inherent in EVERY painful situation you will ever face.

Here is the key...

You must come from Bliss in order to transcend suffering. Do not waste any effort trying to avoid or suppress pain. Pain is a natural part of Life. Refrain from grabbing onto the pain as if it were an old comfy coat that warms and holds you in its familiar clutches.

Instead, come from Bliss.

Come from the decision to remain Open and Free in the moment-to-moment Bliss that ripples underneath all things. It is very simple. Make a choice to release your suffering and allow your Magnificence to emerge.

Thank You For Leaving Me is a transmission of thoughts that will unbind you, if you allow it. It is an example of how one chooses peace over pain, joy over sorrow. It is a manual on How to Live from your Essence.

Farhana understands how to permanently cross the abyss between dark suffering and lasting Happiness. She uses her story to show the power of choice, vulnerability, humor, discipline and Truth. The opportunity lies for you to do the same.

As you re-read passages, read it with the eyes of your Heart and allow your game to be cracked open by the words. Reveal the joyful, relaxed, and capable YOU that has been there all along.

Let this nourish your Soul. Embrace the Freedom that is already yours.

Great Love and Gratitude to Farhana for bringing us these candid words of instruction and Wisdom. May they be a blessing to you.

Blessings,
Satyen Raja
Relationship Transformation Guru

Author's Note

We've all heard that time heals all wounds.

It's true... if we let it.

In the beginning, birthdays, anniversaries and other holidays become opportunities for me to reflect and gauge how I was doing. In essence, it was like I was checking my temperature along the way. Sometimes it was liberating, sometimes painful. In the beginning, it was both.

I did not notice until my editor pointed it out, that today, the day that I hand in my manuscript, is my wedding anniversary.

Say what? It appears, I have hit another milestone. I am no longer gauging my existence on this backdrop of "us."

Yes, time eventually does heal all wounds… and, gratitude for the experience heals it faster.

Thank you… for loving you enough to leave me.
Thank *you*… for loving me enough to leave me.

Thank you for leaving me.

About the Author

Farhana Dhalla holds a Business Administration / Marketing degree from SAIT in Calgary Alberta, Canada. She began her career in the corporate world designing leader training programs for Top 100 Companies, and then worked as an Instructor for *Dale Carnegie Training*.

She is a member of eWomen Network—an international organization for professional women, and a founding member of the Evolutionary Business Council. She is a popular guest on radio and television talk shows, and speaks to audience around the world. Farhana is the mother of 3 children.

Stay Connected

Share your thoughts about the book on our Facebook Page "Thank You for Leaving Me"

Visit:
www.FarhanaDhalla.com
www.ThankYouForLeavingMe.com

For information about the author's consulting or speaking venues, contact: info@FarhanaDhalla.com

Other Books by
Bettie Youngs Book Publishers

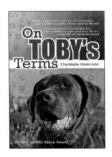

On Toby's Terms

Charmaine Hammond

On Toby's Terms is an endearing story of a beguiling creature who teaches his owners that, despite their trying to teach him how to be the dog they want, he is the one to lay out the terms of being the dog he needs to be. This insight would change their lives forever.

"Simply a beautiful book about life, love, and purpose."
—Jack Canfield, compiler, *Chicken Soup for the Soul* series

"In a perfect world, every dog would have a home and every home would have a dog like Toby!" **—Nina Siemaszko, actress, *The West Wing***

"This is a captivating, heartwarming story and we are very excited about bringing it to film." **—Steve Hudis, Producer**

ISBN: 978-0-9843081-4-9 • ePub: 978-1-936332-15-1 • $15.95

The Maybelline Story

And the Spirited Family Dynasty Behind It

Sharrie Williams

Throughout the twentieth century, Maybelline inflated, collapsed, endured, and thrived in tandem with the nation's upheavals. Williams, to avoid unwanted scrutiny of his private life, cloistered himself behind the gates of his Rudolph Valentino Villa and ran his empire from a distance. This never before told story celebrates the life of a man whose vision rocketed him to success along with the woman held in his orbit: his brother's wife, Evelyn Boecher— who became his lifelong fascination and muse. A fascinating and inspiring story, a tale both epic and intimate, alive with the clash, the hustle, the music, and dance of American enterprise.

"A richly told story of a forty-year, white-hot love triangle that fans the flames of a major worldwide conglomerate."

—Neil Shulman, Associate Producer, *Doc Hollywood*

"Salacious! Engrossing! There are certain stories, so dramatic, so sordid, that they seem positively destined for film; this is one of them." **—*New York Post***

ISBN: 978-0-9843081-1-8 • ePub: 978-1-936332-17-15 • $18.95

The Count, My Mother, and Me

Jane Congdon

The terrifying legend of Count Dracula silently skulking through the Transylvania night may have terrified generations of filmgoers, but the tall, elegant vampire captivated and electrified a young Jane Congdon, igniting a dream to one day see his mysterious land of ancient castles and misty hollows. Four decades later she finally takes her long-awaited trip—never dreaming that it would unearth decades-buried memories, and trigger a life-changing inner journey.

A memoir full of surprises, Jane's story is one of hope, love—and second chances.

"Unfinished business can surface when we least expect it. *It Started with Dracula* is the inspiring story of two parallel journeys: one a carefully planned vacation and the other an astonishing and unexpected detour in healing a wounded heart."
—Charles Whitfield, MD, bestselling author of *Healing the Child Within*

"An elegantly written and cleverly told story. An electrifying read."
—Diane Bruno, CISION Media

ISBN: 978-1-936332-10-6 • ePub: 978-1-936332-11-3 • $15.95

The Rebirth of Suzzan Blac

Suzzan Blac

A horrific upbringing and then abduction into the sex slave industry would all but kill Suzzan's spirit to live. But a happy marriage and two children brought love—and forty-two stunning paintings, art so raw that it initially frightened even the artist. "I hid the pieces for 15 years," says Suzzan, "but just as with the secrets in this book, I am slowing sneaking them out, one by one by one." Now a renowned artist, her work is exhibited world-wide.

A story of inspiration, truth and victory.

"A solid memoir about a life reconstructed. Chilling, thrilling, and thought provoking."
—Pearry Teo, Producer, *The Gene Generation*

ISBN: 978-1-936332-22-9 • ePub: 978-1-936332-23-6 • $16.95

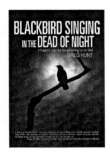

Blackbird Singing in the Dead of Night

What to Do When God Won't Answer

Gregory L. Hunt

Pastor Greg Hunt had devoted nearly thirty years to congregational ministry, helping people experience God and find their way in life. Then came his own crisis of faith and calling. While turning to God for guidance, he finds nothing. Neither his education nor his religious involvements could prepare him for the disorienting impact of the experience.

Alarmed, he tries an experiment. The result is startling—and changes his life entirely.

"In this most beautiful memoir, Greg Hunt invites us into an unsettling time in his life, exposes the fault lines of his faith, and describes the path he walked into and out of the dark. Thanks to the trail markers he leaves along the way, he makes it easier for us to find our way, too."

—Susan M. Heim, co-author, *Chicken Soup for the Soul,*
Devotional Stories for Women

"Compelling. If you have ever longed to hear God whispering a love song into your life, read this book."

—Gary Chapman, *NY Times* bestselling author, *The Love Languages of God*

ISBN: 978-1-936332-07-6 • ePub: 978-1-936332-18-2 • $15.95

DON CARINA

WWII Mafia Heroine

Ron Russell

A father's death in Southern Italy in the 1930s—a place where women who can read are considered unfit for marriage—thrusts seventeen-year-old Carina into servitude as a "black widow," a legal head of the household who cares for her twelve siblings. A scandal forces her into a marriage to Russo, the "Prince of Naples."

By cunning force, Carina seizes control of Russo's organization and disguising herself as a man, controls the most powerful of Mafia groups for nearly a decade. Discovery is inevitable: Interpol has been watching. Nevertheless, Carina survives to tell her children her stunning story of strength and survival.

"A woman as the head of the Mafia, who shows her family her resourcefulness, strength and survival techniques. Unique, creative and powerful! This exciting book blends history, intrigue and power into one delicious epic adventure that you will not want to put down!"
—Linda Gray, Actress, *Dallas*

ISBN: 978-0-9843081-9-4 • ePub: 978-1-936332-49-6 • $15.95

Living with Multiple Personalities

The Christine Ducommun Story

Christine Ducommun

Christine Ducommun was a happily married wife and mother of two, when—after moving back into her childhood home—she began to experience panic attacks and a series of bizarre flashbacks. Eventually diagnosed with Dissociative Identity Disorder (DID), Christine's story details an extraordinary twelve-year ordeal unraveling the buried trauma of her past and the daunting path she must take to heal from it.

Therapy helps to identify Christine's personalities and understand how each helped her cope with her childhood, but she'll need to understand their influence on her adult life. Fully reawakened and present, the personalities compete for control of Christine's mind as she bravely struggles to maintain a stable home for her growing children. In the shadows, her life tailspins into unimaginable chaos—bouts of drinking and drug abuse, sexual escapades, theft and fraud—leaving her to believe she may very well be losing the battle for her sanity. Nearing the point of surrender, a breakthrough brings integration.

A brave story of identity, hope, healing and love.

"Reminiscent of the Academy Award-winning *A Beautiful Mind,* this true story will have you on the edge of your seat. Spellbinding!"   **—Josh Miller, Producer**

ISBN: 978-0-9843081-5-6 • ePub: 978-1-936332-06-9 • $15.95

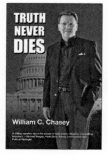

Truth Never Dies

William C. Chasey

A lobbyist for some 40 years, William C. Chasey represented some of the world's most prestigious business clients and twenty-three foreign governments before the US Congress. His integrity never questioned.

All that changed when Chasey was hired to forge communications between Libya and the US Congress. A trip he took with a US Congressman for discussions with then Libyan leader Muammar Qadhafi forever changed Chasey's life. Upon his return, his bank accounts were frozen, clients and friends had been advised not to take his calls.

Things got worse: the CIA, FBI, IRS, and the Federal Judiciary attempted to coerce him into using his unique Libyan access to participate in a CIA-sponsored assassination plot of the two Libyans indicted for the bombing of Pan Am flight 103. Chasey's refusal to cooperate resulted in the destruction of his reputation, a six-year FBI investigation and sting operation, financial ruin, criminal charges, and incarceration in federal prison.

"A somber tale, a thrilling read."   **—Gary Chafetz, author *The Search for the Lost Army***

ISBN: 978-1-936332-46-5 • ePub: 978-1-936332-47-2 • $24.95

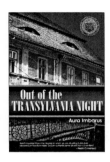

Out of the Transylvania Night

Aura Imbarus

A Pulitzer-Prize entry

"I'd grown up in the land of Transylvania, homeland to Dracula, Vlad the Impaler, and worse, dictator Nicolae Ceausescu," writes the author. "Under his rule, like vampires, we came to life after sundown, hiding our heirloom jewels and documents deep in the earth." Fleeing to the US to rebuild her life, she discovers a startling truth about straddling two cultures and striking a balance between one's dreams and the sacrifices that allow a sense of "home."

"Aura's courage shows the degree to which we are all willing to live lives centered on freedom, hope, and an authentic sense of self. Truly a love story!"
—Nadia Comaneci, Olympic Champion

"A stunning account of erasing a past, but not an identity."
—Todd Greenfield, 20th Century Fox

ISBN: 978-0-9843081-2-5 • ePub: 978-1-936332-20-5 • $14.95

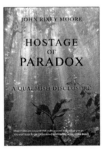

Hostage of Paradox

A Qualmish Disclosure

John Rixey Moore

Few people then or now know about the clandestine war that the CIA ran in Vietnam, using the Green Berets for secret operations throughout Southeast Asia.

This was not the Vietnam War of the newsreels, the body counts, rice paddy footage, and men smoking cigarettes on the sandbag bunkers. This was a shadow directive of deep-penetration interdiction, reconnaissance, and assassination missions conducted by a selected few Special Forces teams, usually consisting of only two Americans and a handful of Chinese mercenaries, called Nungs.

These specialized units deployed quietly from forward operations bases to prowl through agendas that, for security reasons, were seldom completely understood by the men themselves.

Hostage of Paradox is the first-hand account by one of these elite team leaders.

"A compelling story told with extraordinary insight, disconcerting reality, and engaging humor."   **—David Hadley, actor, *China Beach***

ISBN: 978-1-936332-37-3 • ePub: 978-1-936332-33-5 • $29.95

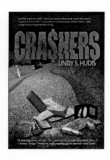

Crashers

A Tale of "Cappers" and "Hammers"

Lindy S. Hudis

The illegal business of fraudulent car accidents is a multi-million dollar racket, involving unscrupulous medical providers, personal injury attorneys, and the cooperating passengers involved in the accidents. Innocent people are often swept into it. Newly engaged Nathan and Shari, who are swimming in mounting debt, were easy prey: seduced by an offer from a stranger to move from hard times to good times in no time, Shari finds herself the "victim" in a staged auto accident. Shari gets her payday, but breaking free of this dark underworld will take nothing short of a miracle.

"A riveting story of love, life—and limits. A non-stop thrill ride."
—Dennis "Danger" Madalone, stunt coordinator, *Castle*

ISBN: 978-1-936332-27-4 • ePub: 978-1-936332-28-1 • $16.95

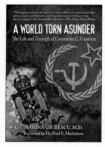

A World Torn Asunder

The Life and Triumph of Constantin C. Giurescu

Marina Giurescu, M.D.

Constantin C. Giurescu was Romania's leading historian and author of the seminal *The History of the Romanian People*. His granddaughter's fascinating story of this remarkable man and his family follows their struggles in war-torn Romania from 1900 to the fall of the Soviet Union. An "enlightened" society is dismantled with the 1946 Communist takeover of Romania, and Constantin is confined to the notorious Sighet penitentiary.

Drawing on her grandfather's prison diary (which was put in a glass jar, buried in a yard, then smuggled out of the country by Dr. Paul E. Michelson—who does the FOREWORD for this book), private letters and her own research, Dr. Giurescu writes of the legacy from the turn of the century to the fall of Communism.

We see the rise of modern Romania, the misery of World War I, the blossoming of its culture between the wars, and then the sellout of Eastern Europe to Russia after World War II. In this sweeping account, we see not only its effects socially and culturally, but the triumph in its wake: a man and his people who reclaim better lives for themselves, and in the process, teach us a lesson in endurance, patience, and will—not only to survive, but to thrive.

"The inspirational story of a quiet man and his silent defiance in the face of tyranny."
—Dr. Connie Mariano, author of *The White House Doctor*

ISBN: 978-1-936332-76-2 • ePub: 978-1-936332-77-9 • $21.95

Electric Living

The Science behind
the Law of Attraction

Kolie Crutcher

Although much has been written about how the Law of Attraction works, Electric Living: The Science Behind the Law of Attraction, is the first book to examine why it works—for good or bad. Skeptics and adherents alike will find Kolie Crutcher's exploration of the science behind this this potent law a fascinating read.

An electrical engineer by training, Crutcher applies his in-depth knowledge of electrical engineering principles and practical engineering experience detailing the scientific explanation of why human beings become what they think. A practical, step-by-step guide to help you harness your thoughts and emotions so that the Law of Attraction will benefit you.

"Electric Living: The Science Behind the Law of Attraction is the real deal when it comes to the Law of Attraction. Kolie's philosophy of Consciousness Creates is the key that unlocks the door to tremendous wealth. This book is a must-read for anyone who wants to be successful in his or her personal or professional life."

—**Freeway Ricky Ross**

ISBN: 978-1-936332-58-8 • ePub: 978-1-936332-59-5 • $16.95

Trafficking the Good Life

Jennifer Myers

Jennifer Myers had worked long and hard toward a successful career as a dancer in Chicago, but just as her star was rising, she fell in love with the kingpin of a drug trafficking operation. Drawn to his life of luxury, she soon became a vital partner in driving marijuana across the country, making unbelievable sums of easy money that she stacked in shoeboxes and spent like an heiress.

Steeped in moral ambiguity, she sought to cleanse her soul with the guidance of spiritual gurus and New Age prophets—to no avail. Only time in a federal prison made her face up to and understand her choices. It was there, at rock bottom, that she discovered that her real prison was the one she had unwittingly made inside herself and where she could start rebuilding a life of purpose and ethical pursuit.

"A gripping memoir. When the DEA finally knocks on Myers's door, she and the reader both see the moment for what it truly is—not so much an arrest as a rescue."
—**Tony D'Souza, author of** *Whiteman and Mule*

"A stunningly honest exploration of a woman finding her way through a very masculine world . . . and finding her voice by facing the choices she has made."
—**Dr. Linda Savage, author of** *Reclaiming Goddess Sexuality*

ISBN: 978-1-936332-67-0 • ePub: 978-1-936332-68-7 • $18.95

Voodoo in My Blood

A Healer's Journey from Surgeon to Shaman

Carolle Jean-Murat, M.D.

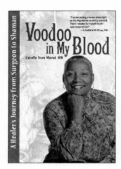

Born and raised in Haiti to a family of healers, US trained physician Carolle Jean-Murat came to be regarded as a world-class surgeon. But her success harbored a secret: in the operating room, she could quickly intuit the root cause of her patient's illness, often times knowing she could help the patient without surgery. Carolle knew that to fellow surgeons, her intuition was best left unmentioned. But when the devastating earthquake hit Haiti and Carolle returned to help, she had to acknowledge the shaman she had become.

"This fascinating memoir sheds light on the importance of asking yourself, 'Have I created for myself the life I've meant to live?'"
> —**Christiane Northrup, M.D., author of the New York Times bestsellers:** *Women's Bodies, Women's Wisdom* **and** *The Wisdom of Menopause*

ISBN: 978-1-936332-05-2 • ePub: 978-1-936332-04-5 • $21.95

Fastest Man in the World

The Tony Volpentest Story

Tony Volpentest

Foreword by Ross Perot

Tony Volpentest, a four-time Paralympic gold medalist and five-time world champion sprinter, is a 2012 nominee for the Olympic Hall of Fame

"This inspiring story is about the thrill of victory to be sure—winning gold—but it is also a reminder about human potential: the willingness to push ourselves beyond the ledge of our own imagination. A powerfully inspirational story."
> —**Charlie Huebner, United States Olympic Committee**

"This is a moving, motivating and inspiring book."
> —**Dan O'Brien, world and Olympic champion decathlete**

"Tony's story shows us that no matter where we start the race, no matter what the obstacles, we all have it within us to reach powerful goals."
> —**Oscar Pistorius, "Blade Runner," double amputee, world record holder in the 100, 200 and 400 meters**

ISBN: 978-1-936332-00-7 • ePub: 978-1-936332-01-4 • $16.95

Amazing Adventures of a Nobody

Leon Logothetis

From the Hit Television Series Aired in 100 Countries!

Tired of his disconnected life and uninspiring job, Leon Logothetis leaves it all behind—job, money, home, even his cell phone—and hits the road with nothing but the clothes on his back and five dollars in his pocket, relying on the kindness of strangers and the serendipity of the open road for his daily keep. Masterful storytelling!

"A gem of a book; endearing, engaging and inspiring."
—Catharine Hamm, Los Angeles Times Travel Editor

"Warm, funny, and entertaining. If you're looking to find meaning in this disconnected world of ours, this book contains many clues." **—Psychology Today**

ISBN: 978-0-9843081-3-2 • ePub: 978-1-936332-51-9 • $14.95

MR. JOE

Tales from a Haunted Life

Joseph Barnett and Jane Congdon

Do you believe in ghosts? Joseph Barnett didn't, until the winter he was fired from his career job and became a school custodian to make ends meet. The fact that the eighty-five-year-old school where he now worked was built near a cemetery had barely registered with Joe when he was assigned the graveyard shift. But soon, walking the dim halls alone at night, listening to the wind howl outside, Joe was confronted with a series of bizarre and terrifying occurrences.

It wasn't just the ghosts of the graveyard shift that haunted him. Once the child of a distant father and an alcoholic mother, now a man devastated by a failed marriage, fearful of succeeding as a single dad, and challenged by an overwhelming illness, Joe is haunted by his own personal ghosts.

The story of Joseph's challenges and triumphs emerges as an eloquent metaphor of ghosts, past and present, real and emotional, and how a man puts his beliefs about self—and ghosts—to the test.

"Thrilling, thoughtful, elegantly told. So much more than a ghost story."
—Cyrus Webb, CEO, Conversation Book Club

"This is truly inspirational work, a very special book—a gift to any reader."
—Diane Bruno, CISION Media

ISBN: 978-1-936332-78-6 • ePub: 978-1-936332-79-3 • $18.95

The Search for the Lost Army
The National Geographic and
Harvard University Expedition

Gary S. Chafetz

In one of history's greatest ancient disasters, a Persian army of 50,000 soldiers was suffocated by a hurricane-force sandstorm in 525 BC in Egypt's Western Desert. No trace of this conquering army, hauling huge quantities of looted gold and silver, has ever surfaced.

Nearly 25 centuries later on October 6, 1981, Egyptian Military Intelligence, the CIA, and Israel's Mossad secretly orchestrated the assassination of President Anwar Sadat, hoping to prevent Egypt's descent—as had befallen Iran two years before—into the hands of Islamic zealots. Because he had made peace with Israel and therefore had become a marked man in Egypt and the Middle East, Sadat had to be sacrificed to preserve the status quo.

These two distant events become intimately interwoven in the story of Alex Goodman, who defeats impossible obstacles as he leads a Harvard University/ National Geographic Society archaeological expedition into Egypt's Great Sand Sea in search of the Lost Army of Cambyses, the demons that haunt him, and the woman he loves. Based on a true story.

Gary Chafetz, referred to as "one of the ten best journalists of the past twenty-five years," is a former Boston Globe correspondent and was twice nominated for a Pulitzer Prize by the Globe.

ISBN: 978-1-936332-98-4 • ePub: 978-1-936332-99-1 • $19.95

The Tortoise Shell Code

V Frank Asaro

Off the coast of Southern California, the Sea Diva, a tuna boat, sinks. Members of the crew are missing and what happened remains a mystery. Anthony Darren, a renowned and wealthy lawyer at the top of his game, knows the boat's owner and soon becomes involved in the case. As the case goes to trial, a missing crew member is believed to be at fault, but new evidence comes to light and the finger of guilt points in a completely unanticipated direction.

Now Anthony must pull together all his resources to find the truth in what has happened and free a wrongly accused man—as well as untangle himself. Fighting despair, he finds that the recent events have called much larger issues into question. As he struggles to right this terrible wrong, Anthony makes new and enlightening discoveries in his own life-long battle for personal and global justice.

V Frank Asaro is a lawyer, musician, composer, inventor and philosopher. He is also the author of Universal Co-opetition.

ISBN: 978-1-936332-60-1 • ePub: 978-1-936332-61-8 • $24.95

Diary of a Beverly Hills Matchmaker

Marla Martenson

Quick-witted Marla takes her readers for a hilarious romp through her days as an LA matchmaker where looks are everything and money talks. The Cupid of Beverly Hills has introduced countless couples who lived happily ever-after, but for every success story there are hysterically funny dating disasters with high-maintenance, out of touch clients. Marla writes with charm and self-effacement about the universal struggle to love and be loved.

"Martenson's irresistible quick wit will have you rolling on the floor."
—Megan Castran, international YouTube queen

ISBN 978-0-9843081-0-1 • ePub: 978-1-936332-03-8 • $14.95

GPS YOUR BEST LIFE

Charting Your Destination and Getting There in Style

Charmaine Hammond and Debra Kasowski

Foreword by Jack Canfield

Obstacles and roadblocks can detour us on the way to success, or even prevent us from getting there at all. GPS Your Best Life helps you determine where you are now, and, through practical strategies and assessments, helps you clarify what you want in your personal and career life, and shows you how to expertly navigate through hidden fears and procrastination so as to get on the road to your best life—now!

A most useful guide to charting and traversing the many options that lay before you.

Charmaine Hammond is the bestselling author of On Toby's Terms, and speaks to audiences around the world. Debra Kasowski is founder and CEO of the Millionaire Woman Club, and a professional speaker.

"A perfect book for servicing your most important vehicle: yourself. No matter where you are in your life, the concepts and direction provided in this book will help you get to a better place. It's a must read."
—Ken Kragen, author of *Life Is a Contact Sport*, and organizer of *We Are the World*, and *Hands Across America*, and other historic humanitarian events

ISBN: 978-1-936332-26-7 • ePub: 978-1-936332-41-0 • $16.95

Universal Co-opetition

Nature's Fusion of
Co-operation and Competition

V Frank Asaro

A key ingredient in business success is competition—and coopera-tion. Too much of one or the other can erode personal and organizational goals. This book identifies and explains the natural, fundamental law that unifies the apparently opposing forces of cooperation and competition.

Finding this synthesis point in a variety of situations—from the personal to the organizational—can save our finances, our family, our future, and our world.

V Frank Asaro is a lawyer, musician, composer, inventor and philosopher. He is also the author of *The Tortoise Shell Code*.

ISBN: 978-1-936332-08-3 • ePub: 978-1-936332-09-0 • $15.95

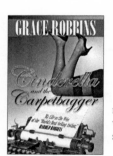

Cinderella
and the Carpetbagger

Grace Robbins

When she pulled The Carpetbaggers off the shelf, looking for a good read to while away the weekend, Grace Palermo never imagined that she would soon meet the book's international best-selling author, let alone spend the next thirty years of her life with him.

When Grace and Harold met, his career was already well established, but over the next thirty years, his fame would become legendary, as did their lifestyle together. This engrossing memoir spans the 60s, 70s, and 80s, in all their hallucinogenic and freewheeling splen-dor. The couple was at the center of a globetrotting jet set, with mansions in Beverly Hills, villas and yachts in the South of France and Acapulco, known for their lavish—and sometimes orgiastic parties. Their life together rivaled that of the characters in Harold's books, but in the privacy of their home things weren't always as they seemed.

Grace Robbins reveals what it was like to live alongside the "prince of sex and scandal," and takes us on a journey of rollicking good fun, be it a chance meeting with Pablo Picasso, a lifetime friendship with James Baldwin, a steamy encounter with a member of the Rat Pack—and a couple of the James Bond men, or a racy evening in Hamburg with composer Frederick Lowe. With charm, introspection, and humor, Grace lays open her fascinating, provocative roller-coaster ride, her true Cinderella tale.

ISBN: 978-0-9882848-2-1 • ePub: 978-0-9882848-4-5 • $28.95

The Girl Who Gave Her Wish Away

Sharon Babineau

Foreword by Graig Kielburger,
Co-Founder, FREE THE CHILDREN

The Children's Wish Foundation approached lovely thirteen-year-old Maddison Babineau just after she received her cancer diagnosis. "You can have anything," they told her, "a Disney cruise? The chance to meet your favorite movie star? A five thousand dollar shopping spree?"

Maddie knew exactly what she wanted. She had recently been moved to tears after watching a television program about the plight of orphaned children in an African village. Maddie's wish? To ease the suffering of these children half-way across the world. Despite the ravishing cancer, she became an indefatigable fundraiser for "her children."

In The Girl Who Gave Wish Away, her mother reveals Maddie's remarkable journey of providing hope and future to the village children who had filled her heart.

A special story, heartwarming and reassuring.

ISBN: 978-1-936332-96-0 • ePub: 978-1-936332-97-7 • $18.95

Company of Stone

John Rixey Moore

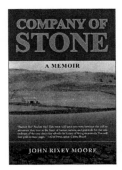

Say what you will, but the spirit of a place takes on an important role in the affairs of humans. Whether in an old house, an empty theater, a cemetery, where there was some past conflict a tangible energy haunts such places, and it can attach itself to a visitor from the present...

With yet unhealed wounds from recent combat in SE Asia, John Moore undertook an unexpected walking tour in the rugged Scottish highlands. With the approach of a season of freezing rainstorms he took shelter in a remote monastery—a chance encounter that would change his future, his beliefs about blind chance, and the unexpected courses by which the best in human nature can smuggle its way into the life of a stranger. He did not anticipate the brotherhood's easy hospitality or the surprising variety of personalities and guarded backgrounds that soon emerged through their silent community.

Afterwards, a chance conversation overheard in a village pub steered him to Canada, where he took a job as a rock drill operator in a large industrial gold mine. The dangers he encountered among the lost men in that dangerous other world, secretive men who sought permanent anonymity in the perils of work deep underground—a brutal kind of monasticism itself—challenged both his endurance and his sense of humanity.

With sensitivity and delightful good humor, Moore explores the surprising lessons learned in these strangely rich fraternities of forgotten men—a brotherhood housed in crumbling medieval masonry, and one shared in the unforgiving depths of the gold mine.

ISBN: 978-1-936332-44-1 • ePub: 978-1-936332-45-8 • $19.95

The Morphine Dream

Don Brown with *Boston Globe Pulitzer nominated Gary S. Chafetz*

An amazing story of one man's loss and gain, hope, and the revealing of an unexpected calling.

At 36, high-school dropout and a failed semi-professional ballplayer Donald Brown hit bottom when an industrial accident left him immobilized. But Brown had a dream while on a morphine drip after surgery: he imagined himself graduating from Harvard Law School (he was a classmate of Barack Obama) and walking across America. Brown realizes both seemingly unreachable goals, and achieves national recognition as a legal crusader for minority homeowners. An intriguing tale of his long walk—both physical and metaphorical.

A story of perseverance and second chances.

"An incredibly inspirational memoir." —**Alan M. Dershowitz, professor, Harvard Law School**

ISBN: 978-1-936332-25-0 • ePub: 978-1-936332-26-7 • $24.95

Bettie Youngs Books

We specialize in MEMOIRS

. . . books that celebrate

fascinating people and

remarkable journeys

In bookstores everywhere, online, Espresso,
or from the publisher, Bettie Youngs Books
VISIT OUR WEBSITE AT
www.BettieYoungsBooks.com
To contact:
info@BettieYoungsBooks.com

CPSIA information can be obtained at www.ICGtesting.com
Printed in the USA
BVOW030906180113

310982BV00001B/2/P